Opposite page.
Joseph Schranz (1760-90)
Mouse island seen from one gun
battery.
Watercolour over pencil
(20.5 x 29 cm).
Private collection.

CORFU

THE GARDEN ISLE

Presented by Spiro Flamburiari

Edited by Frank Giles

with photographs by Fritz von der Schulenburg and Christopher Simon Sykes

*Published by John Murray in association with
The Hellenic Group of Companies Ltd.
and Abbeville Press.*

This book is dedicated
to a very special lady

My Wife

It is also a tribute
to the memory of my dear Mother

Copyright ©1994 S. L. Flamburiari
ISBN 0-7195-5375-X John Murray (UK)
ISBN 1-55859-845-6 Abbeville Press (USA)

First Edition

Designed by Ken Reilly

Artwork by Precision Presentation

Photographs: Fritz von der Schulenburg and
Christopher Simon Sykes

Edited by Frank Giles

Printed and Bound in Italy by
Amilcare Pizzi s.p.a.

First published in 1994 by
John Murray (Publishers) Ltd
50 Albemarle Street, London W1X 4BD
in association with
The Hellenic Group of Companies Ltd
2 Montpelier Mews, London SW7 1HB
and
Abbeville Press
488 Madison Avenue, New York NY 10022

We are grateful for
the interest and support
given to this book
by our sponsors:

Aspis Pronia Insurance

*

The Cavalieri Hotel, Corfu

*

Mr John Karageorgis
and
Silver Carriers

*

The Greek Ministry of Tourism

Contents

HRH The Duke of Kent, KG

It is with pride and pleasure that I respond to the invitation to contribute a foreword to
this fine book about Corfu: pride because my mother, the youngest daughter of Prince Nicholas
of Greece, was a Princess of Greece; pleasure because of the memories of happy holidays
that I and my family have spent on the island.

As some of the essays in the book point out, Corfu's long and eventful history has given it
a unique flavour. The most westerly outpost of Greece, it has a natural affinity with the countries
of Western Europe. Yet no one can spend any time in the island without quickly realising
that its soul is Greek. This fusion of the two traditions, Eastern and Western, is what gives Corfu
its special appeal, experienced by so many travellers over the years.

I wish I knew the island better and could speak more than a few halting words of Greek.
But one does not have to be a fluent Greek speaker to sense the warmth of welcome and
generosity of spirit which the ordinary people of Corfu extend to their foreign guests.
No doubt the same is true of other parts of Greece, where hospitality to the stranger is part of
the way of life. But in a book about Corfu it is, I think, appropriate to stress this personal
side of the Ionian temperament, which is happily unchanging.

It is a source of satisfaction to me, with my Anglo-Greek ancestry, to think that for nearly
half a century Britain was the protecting power of the Ionian islands. Her rule may not perhaps have
been agreeable to everyone, but she brought many benefits, some of them still apparent today.
If in the end the islanders preferred to be ruled by Greece, that was only natural.
When the British did voluntarily withdraw in the 1860s, they did so with good grace and as friends.
The countless numbers of them - perhaps too many - who today choose Corfu for their holidays
are vivid proof that friendship endures and that the island continues to cast its inimitable spell.

I hope that this book will bring pleasure to many people, whether they know Corfu or not,
and I wish it and those who have helped to create it good luck with their venture.

Contributors

1. Spiro Flamburiari,

who is the creator of this book, was born in Corfu. He has been involved over the years with a number of major Tourist and Leisure Developments in Corfu, other parts of Greece and the USA. He is considered an authority on International Tourism and has contributed a number of essays on this subject. His main hobby is devoted to the collection of watercolours on subjects related mainly to Corfu, the Ionian Islands and Greece. His involvement with Corfu - where he spends his holidays with his wife in their villa by the sea - is an ongoing affair.

2. Frank Giles,

who has both edited and contributed to the book, is a former Editor of the Sunday Times and the author of several books. In 1972 he and his wife bought some land at the north-east corner of Corfu and built a small house which they visit twice annually.

3. John Julius Norwich,

was born in 1929, son of the statesman and diplomat Alfred Duff Cooper and the Lady Diana Cooper. Educated at Upper Canada College Toronto, Eton, the University of Strasburg and New College Oxford, he spent twelve years in H.M. Foreign Service and in 1964 resigned to become a writer. His books include: "The Normans in Sicily", "Mount Athos", "A History of Venice", "The Architecture of Southern England"and the first two volumes of a three volume history of the Byzantine Empire. John Julius Norwich has worked on radio and has written some thirty historical documentary films for TV. In 1993, after being Curator of the exhibition 'Sovereign' at the Victoria and Albert Museum, he was appointed Commander of the Royal Victorian Order. Chairman of the Venice in Peril Fund, he is a lecturer on art-historical, architectural and musical subjects in Britain and N. America.

4.(1) Andrew Sinclair

is a well known historian and writer who lived in a Venetian villa at Kombitsi in Corfu for twenty years. His translation of the Greek Anthology was much praised by the late Sir William Golding. He is married to the writer Sonia Melchett.
Andrew Sinclair achieved immediate recognition with his first novel, "The Breaking of Bumbo". Subsequent books include biographies of Jack London, John Ford, and more recently, Francis Bacon. Andrew Sinclair has also written other works of fiction and the screenplay for Dylan Thomas's "Under Milk Wood".

4.(2) Lord Michael Pratt

is the author of "Britain's Greek Empire", a history of the Ionian islands with special emphasis on the years of the British Protectorate. His latest work on the country houses of Central Europe has been widely acclaimed.

5. Countess Mildred Flamburiari

has written and illustrated a book of children's stories and has contributed articles to various magazines. Since her marriage to Spiro Flamburiari she has been involved with Corfu in many ways. She is an accomplished artist and has exhibited her paintings in a one-woman show.

6. Major J.K. Forte MBE

is the author of 5 well reviewed books about Corfu and one on old Paxos. He first visited Corfu in 1946. In 1947 he married Nadia, great-grand-daughter of Sir Demetrius Curcumelli, Regent of Corfu at the time the Ionian Islands were seceded to Greece. In 1958 he was appointed British Vice-Consul in Corfu, a post he held until 1971. He is probably best remembered for resuscitating Corfu cricket, for saving the Anglican Church of Holy Trinity from extinction, and for his acclaimed guide book "Corfu ,Venus of the Isles".

7. Gerald Durrell,

writer, broadcaster, traveller, film maker, zoologist and founder of Jersey Zoological Park, now lives in Jersey. His special relationship with Corfu derives from his memories of childhood there, enshrined in several books of which the best known is "My Family and Other Animals".

8. Aphrodite Agoropoulou-Birbili

is an Assistant Professor of History of Architecture at the National Technical University of Athens. She has published various books and monographs including "The architecture of the town of Corfu during the dominion of the Venetian Republic" (Athens 1976), "Kerkyra, Greek traditional architecture" (Athens 1982) and "The work of the Kerkyran architect John Chronis" (Corfu 1983).

9. Evita Arapoglou

is an art historian specialising in l9th and early 20th century Greek art. She has organised various exhibitions and lectured on her subject in England, Greece and Cyprus. She is the author of two books: "The A.G. Leventis Collection of l9th and 20th century Greek Paintings" (1989) and "Ghika - Drawings" (1992).

10. Peter Nahum

has rightly been credited as father of the modern Victorian art market. As director of Sotheby's Belgravia from its inception in 1971 to its close in 1984, he was responsible for bringing to the public accessible and exciting images in scholarly catalogues. More recently, as a dealer in St James's, he is recognised as the leading expert in his field and is consulted by museums and major collectors worldwide. He has also published books on the subject. He believes that we should celebrate artists such as Edward Lear who, by leading a fugitive, itinerant life from his own unhappiness, has given successive generations such pleasure.

11. Helena Matheopoulos

was born in Athens and has lived in England for most of her life. She has degrees in medieval history from London University and has worked as a journalist, first as Fashion Editor for the Tatler *and the* Daily Express, *and subsequently in the fields of arts and music, as a contributor to the London* Evening News, *the* Sunday Times, Observer, Gramophone *and* Opera Now. *Her first book, "Maestro: Encounters with Conductors Today", was published in 1982 and was followed by "Bravo" (1986) and "Diva" (1991).*

12. Ann Nash,

who, with her ex-Royal Navy husband, has lived in Corfu for many years, is an expert on its flora and fauna. She has led many groups of visiting flower-lovers up the hills and down the valleys she knows so well in search of floral and arboreal treasures.

13. Fritz von der Schulenburg and Christopher Simon Sykes

are both photographers of international acclaim and both specialists of landscape and interiors of some of the world's most famous houses.

14. Lord Orr-Ewing

was educated at Harrow and Trinity College Oxford where he graduated in physics. He has always been a keen cricketer and, after war service in the RAF, was appointed as Manager of BBC Television Outside Broadcasts. In this capacity he recruited the late Brian Johnston as a cricket commentator.
In 1950 he entered politics and was elected Member of Parliament for Hendon North. Having served as a Minister in the Macmillan administration, he joined the House of Lords in 1970 where he continues to play an active role. His hobbies include cricket, tennis and skiing and he has for many years led the Lords and Commons joint skiing team. During numerous family visits to Corfu over the last 30 years he encouraged and supported cricket on the island and is responsible for creating the Anglo-Corfu Cricket Association (ACCA) of which he is President.

15. Augustus Sordinas

is a Professor at the Ionian University and an authority on the history of the island's olive-oil mills and presses and oil production. He is the owner of Kothoniki, the historic house described in Chapter 5.

1 *Introduction*

Spiro Flamburiari

The idea of introducing Corfu 'in text and pictures' has been in my mind for a very long time. One needed, of course, to put together as much material as possible in order to achieve this goal. But more than just the material, one needed passion and encouragement. The passion, I guess, was always there; it was inherited from my parents whose love for my native island was overwhelmingly strong.

The encouragement to create this book came from various sources. Firstly from my dear wife, and then from the Orr-Ewing family whose association with Corfu goes back many years. In particular my long standing friend and partner, Simon Orr-Ewing, has played a significant role in convincing me to go ahead with this venture.... But more than anybody else, the enthusiasm of Andrew Sinclair sealed my decision. And so this

book was born. In fact, one can truthfully say that this is the result of my love for this magic island!

Although I left Corfu as a young boy, I have somehow been connected with it over the years almost constantly. This does not surprise me; it only confirms once more what Edward Lear wrote in March, 1863:

"......the more I see of this place, so the more I feel that no other spot on earth can be fuller of beauty, and of variety of beauty..."

In the pages which follow, a number of well known writers, every one an expert in his own field, lovers of Corfu, together with two brilliant photographers and an excellent book designer under the skilled editorship of Frank Giles present 'in text and pictures' my tribute to this special Garden Isle.

Edward Lear (1812-1888)
View from the Benitza Road, near
Gastouri - Corfu
Signed with initials ;
Oil on canvas 13.5 x 12.5 inches
By kind permission of
Peter Nahum at the Leicester
Galleries, London.

A fine view across the water of the fortress and town of Corfu painted by the nineteenth century Corfiot watercolourist Angelos Giallinas. Private collection.

2 *Prologue*

Frank Giles

This book is the story, in text and pictures, of the principal Ionian island whose very name the Victorian painter Edward Lear could not bring himself to write "without a pang" when he left it. Other visitors have felt the same irresistible attraction, vowing to return to this green and lovely place. It is not merely the extraordinary beauty of the island that exerts so powerful a spell. There is also its unique place in history and geography as the crossroads of the Eastern Mediterranean, where for many centuries races and cultures have been meeting and mixing.

Unlike the rest of Greece and (intermittently) some of the other Ionian Islands, Corfu never fell under the Ottoman yoke, despite two vigorous attempts by the Turks to conquer it. Consequently it has, under the successive rule of the Venetians, the French and the British, developed a role that makes it seem more a part of the Western than the Levantine world. This impression, while generally true, is also deceptive. For despite its Western affiliations, Corfu has never ceased culturally to be Greek. Running right through the island's long and chequered history are the twin threads of the Greek Orthodox Church and the Greek language.

Typical of the dual nature of Corfiot history and society is Corfu town itself, one of the most picturesque cities of the Mediterranean world. Its palaces, fortresses, tiny alleyways and wide main streets, its faded stucco and shuttered façades, its lines of drying washing, its well-heads set in secluded little squares and angles: all bear eloquent witness to its earlier history. The visitor could think him - or herself in Genoa or Naples. Then round the corner comes a black-robed, stovepipe-hatted Orthodox priest, and at his passing old ladies cross themselves fervently and with rapid gestures, three fingers to denote the Trinity, the right shoulder touched before the left. This is the world of Byzantium, experienced moreover against the breath-taking backdrop, seen across the cobalt waters of the Ionian Sea, of the mountains of northern Epirus, snow-capped in winter and shrouded in a purple haze in summer and autumn.

Edward Lear, writing in 1857, could hardly contain his descriptive flow: "anything like the splendour of olive-grove and orange-garden, the blue of sky and ivory of church and chapel, the violet of mountain, rising from peacock-wing-hued sea, and tipped with lines of silver snow, can hardly be imagined". Lear, like other artists of foreign and Corfiot origin, has left ample pictorial evidence for his enthusiasm.

Much of what they saw and painted has changed today. The passage of the years and the coming of mass tourism has seen to that. But much of the charm remains. The vast olive-groves, planted in Venetian times, still account for a large part of the island's vegetation and are laboriously harvested for some of the world's finest oil. Nor can any modern development alter the quality of the light: not the brilliant, eye-aching clarity of the Aegean, but something altogether softer, more romantic and varied, calling to mind on certain days the lambent nature of the sky over the Western Isles of Scotland, on others the shimmer of the Bay of Naples at sunset.

The aim of this book, designed for Corfiots and non-Corfiots alike, is to evoke the spirit of the distant and not so distant past, drawing upon literary, historical, artistic and botanical sources, while at the same time giving something of the flavour of the island today, which still has a strong claim to the accolade, bestowed by Gerald Durrell in the title of one of his books, of "The Garden of the Gods".

3 A Voyage over the Years

John Julius Norwich

Ulysses' arrival in Corfu was delayed - indeed, very nearly prevented - by the fury of Poseidon, who stirred up a great tempest that shattered his ship to matchwood. At last, however, he struggled ashore and, in one of the most celebrated scenes in all Homer, found the white-armed princess Nausicaa and her handmaidens playing ball on the beach. She told him of her island and of its people, "who have no use for the bow and quiver, but spend their energy on masts and oars and on the graceful craft they love to sail across the foam-flecked seas"; and, as she spoke, she introduced Corfu into history, literature, and the civilisation of Europe.

It is a pretty story - prettier by far (and a good deal more believable) than the grim legend according to which the island is nothing less than the sickle with which Kronos - better known to us as Saturn - somewhat ungratefully emasculated his father Uranus, whose descended testicles petrified into the two huge rocks on the promontory of the Old Fort. These "twin peaks"- in Greek, Koryphai - are said to be the origin of the name Corfu, an ugly and oddly oriental-sounding word to my ear, and worse still when the staff of British Airways pronounce it *Corfew*; why, I have often thought, could we not revert to the modern Greek *Kerkyra*, a name that whispers like the wind through the olive-trees or the ripples on the shore?

Old Corfu hands will argue for hours over the precise point at which Ulysses made his landfall. Fortunately, we shall never know; some mysteries are better left unrevealed. The fact is that although the island played an active and even mildly distinguished part in the history of antiquity - apart from anything else, the Corfiots are credited with having won the first sea-battle ever recorded, against the Corinthians in 660 BC - it has failed to preserve more than a handful of classical monuments. This is perhaps not altogether surprising: its position was too

A view of the old fortress showing the remains of the Anemomilos (windmill) from Garitsa bay as it was in the nineteenth century. Watercolour by Angelos Gaillinas. Private collection.

Opposite page. A moonlit scene on the coast facing Albania.

Four times a year the body of Saint Spyridon, held upright in its silver casket, is paraded around Corfu town. This picture shows accompanying priests in their jewel coloured robes.

Opposite page. Saint Spyridon's silver casket reposing in the famous church of his name surrounded by votive offerings.

important at the gateway to the Adriatic and too vulnerable in its proximity to the mainland to allow it to enjoy peace for long. No wonder that in 229 BC it voluntarily surrendered to the Romans, thus beginning that 2,000-year association with Western Europe which has had so remarkably little effect on its character. Soon afterwards, it became a popular Mediterranean staging-post. There Cato met Cicero; both Julius Caesar and Pompey revictualled their opposing fleets; Mark Antony, Levant-bound, said his last farewells to his unhappy wife Octavia; Nero gave one of his more excruciating performances before the altar of Jupiter at Kassiopi; and the Emperor Titus, also on his way to the East, presided with ill-concealed impatience at the interminable games that were organised in his honour.

For the Corfiots, meanwhile, life went on much as it always had, with no major disruption until the arrival, in the late first century AD, of Saints Jason and Sosipatros, disciples of St Paul, to turn them into Christians. The two missionaries ended up in a silver vat of boiling oil; but their work went on, and Corfu had long been a Christian island by the time Constantine the Great summoned the first great Ecumenical Council of the Church at Nicaea in 325. It was here that the young Spyridon, Bishop of Trimython in Cyprus, performed a minor miracle

by causing a brick to spout fire and water, thus proving - if a trifle obscurely - the truth of the doctrine of the Trinity. The action, among many others, earned him a halo, and for the next millennium his uncorrupted body was venerated, first in Cyprus and later in Constantinople. After the fall of that city to the Turks in 1453 Spyridon was brought by stages to Corfu, where he has remained ever since, the island's beloved patron saint. Four times a year he is carried in jubilant procession through the town; on Christmas Eve he is formally enthroned in his church to receive the homage of the faithful.

During the Middle Ages Corfu once again paid the price of her strategic position, being fought over again and again by the Byzantines (to whom, as a former part of the Roman Empire, she rightly belonged), the Normans of South Italy and Sicily under their great adventurer-prince Robert Guiscard, the Greek Principality of Epirus and the Angevins of Naples. Finally, in 1386, she voluntarily accepted the protection of Venice - much as she had that of the Romans sixteen hundred years before; and she was to remain under the banner of St Mark until the downfall of the Most Serene Republic at the hands of the young Napoleon in 1797. The Venetians ringed her with tremendous

PAX | EVAN
TIBI | GELIS
MAR | TA
CE | MEUS

D. O. M.

ALOYSIUS MOCENICO VENETIARUM DUX

MARCUS ANTONIUS DIEDO MODERAT^R SUPREMUS

GEORGIUS GRIMANI CLASSIS PRÆFECTUS

HÆC PRIMUS IUSSIT.

ALTER DISPOSUIT,

TERTIUS NOCTUDIURNO LABORE BREVIT^R ABSOLVIT

fortifications - including the vast New Fortress that still scowls over the harbour - and it was a good thing that they did, since without these the island could never have withstood the two fearsome sieges of 1537 and 1716, by which the Turks sought to incorporate it into the Ottoman Empire.

In both these sieges, it must be admitted, the weather played a considerable part. Corfu has always been famous for the ferocity of its storms, but those that burst upon the island in the early days of September 1537 seem to have been exceptional even by local standards. The cannon became immovable in the mud; dysentery and malaria raged through the Ottoman army, and after barely three weeks' siege it gave up the struggle. In August 1716 the tempest was even worse; within a matter of hours the entire Turkish camp was reduced to a quagmire, the trenches had become canals, the tents had been torn to ribbons or, their guy-ropes snapped like thread, carried off by the gale.

High Commissioners - with a heavy and frequently patronising hand. Their principal inanimate benefactions to Corfu were the city water supply, an admirable network of roads and the two more dubious blessings of ginger beer - *tsin-tsin birra* - and cricket. (Foreign cricketers coming to the island should however be warned: according to Lawrence Durrell - writing in the 1930s - the cry of "How's that?" has come to mean "Out".) But the growing desire of the islanders to be united with Greece, by now an independent monarchy, led in 1864 to a British withdrawal and *enosis.* The islands have remained Greek to the present day.

Greek, Roman, Byzantine, Angevin, Venetian, French, Turkish, Russian, British and finally Greek again: with so kaleidoscopic a history it is hardly surprising that, of all the isles of Greece, Corfu should be the most Westernised - more so even than her Ionian neighbours, since she is more populous and more cultivated than they. But most of her successive overlords have left little mark; only the Venetians ever really succeeded in putting a permanent stamp upon her - above all by their fortifications, though from time to time a delicate fountain, a Latin inscription, a crumbling palace or a winged lion of St Mark, worn but still to be recognised, brings back an unmistakable whiff of the Rialto.

Strangely enough, it hardly seems to matter. Greece has always been a spirit rather than a nation. In the days of antiquity, of those countless independent or semi-independent city-states that made up what we think of as Ancient Greece, nationhood was unknown and undreamt-of. In later centuries the Byzantines, Greek as they may have been, prided themselves on their Roman origins and saw their Empire as being all-embracing, universal under God.

Later, between the fall of Constantinople to the Turks in May 1453 and proclamation of the Greek state in January 1822, there was no Greek nation at all, yet Hellenism survived, as impassioned as ever it had been. Corfu may be of the Adriatic rather than the Aegean, Greece's furthest fingertip reaching out towards the West; yet her spirit remains as it has always remained, Greek through and through. And it is of that spirit, as much as of the beauty of Greece's loveliest island, the richness of its heritage and the nobility of its people, that this book is a celebration.

After the surrender by Venice to Napoleon, Corfu was ruled successively by the French, the Russians and Ottomans and then by the French again, until in 1815 the Treaty of Paris recognised the islands as being once more an independent state, but this time under the protection of the British Crown. Their independence in fact proved more apparent than real, since the British governed the islands - under a series of Lord

4 History

1 The Early Period

Andrew Sinclair

The harbour of Corfu with the old fortress in the background. Watercolour by Joseph Cartwright. Private collection.

The placing of islands makes them accidents of history. Corcyra (now Kerkyra) or Corfu with its magnificent harbour was set to dominate the sea traffic of the Adriatic, the giant sleeve of water that passes the trade of North Africa and the Levant up to Northern Europe. After primitive men had taken to boats and had begun to exchange goods with each other, Corfu would become a haven and a market. Its location would always threaten its independence. It would usually be the base of a Mediterranean commercial empire. Where you are put determines who and what you are.

A subterranean shift of the tectonic plates beneath the crust of the earth - or the hand of Zeus and Neptune - made Corfu into an island, severing it shortly from the mainland of Europe, where the mountains would still quiver and rage with earthquakes and the odd volcano. Palaeolithic and neolithic communities lived in the caves of Corfu near Gardiki and Lake Korission in the south and west. Fossilised bones of extinct animals are still to be found alongside the flint arrowpoints which killed them. These early hunters became gatherers, and the distinctive neolithic pottery discovered at Sidari in the north of the island shows some cultivation and herding five thousand years before Christ, while Bronze Age remains at Ermones prove an abiding population. Fishbones also suggest the harvest of the deep, that had to be crossed before Corfu could become the sea power that it was set to be.

Because of its strategic importance, Corfu was to become the cause of the struggle that destroyed ancient Hellas, the Peloponnesian War of 431-404BC, so well chronicled by the admirable Thucydides the Athenian. He gave the earliest rational description of the ancient societies of the Greeks in their progress from the cavern to the field to the city. There was no settled population, only a series of migrations forced by stronger invaders. "There was no commerce and no safe contacts by land and sea. They only took from their land what they had to produce. There was nothing left over to invest and no regular system of agriculture, because they had no fortifications. At any moment, an invader might come and take away their land from them." They were ready to move, and so they built no cities of any size. They were people ready to be displaced.

Thucydides makes it clear that there was not a record of any action taken by Hellas as a whole before the Trojan War. We now have some evidence from archaeology, but little. According to the later historian Strabo, people called the Liburnians were perhaps the first inhabitants of Corfu. With their primitive warships, the Eretrians from Euboea conquered the island, a part of the Dorian invasion of Greece. Their reign was not long, for they were superseded by the new naval power in Greece, the Corinthians on their vital isthmus of trade. Thucydides ascribed to King Minos of the Cyclades the original Greek-organised fleet, the reduction of piracy and the planting of maritime colonies; but he recognised Corinth as the mother city of Corcyra or Corfu. "As seafaring became more general," he wrote, "and money was accumulated, new cities with walls were built upon the coasts, and the isthmuses were occupied that could trade and defend themselves against local attackers. Those who lived on the coasts could now acquire wealth and live in some security."

At the time of the Trojan War, when Corfu entered into bardic history, there were probably fortified settlements at least on two small peninsulas, at Kanoni by the great harbour of Corfu and at Lefkimmi in the south. Although there is no mention of the islanders on Homer's list of ships in *The Iliad*, in *The Odyssey* Homer's Scheria can only be Corfu, looking "like a shield laid on a misty sea," its boss as Mount Pantokrator and its rim the shores of the sloping land around the peak. So Thucydides and Strabo believed, as did the Corfiots, holding themselves primarily to be the heirs of King Alcinous and the civilised Phaeaceans. As for Ulysses, shipwrecked there and finding Nausicaa and her maidens playing ball on the beach, he found himself in a paradise of welcome and was transported to Ithaca on a superior craft, which may have derived from an ancient Phoenician ship with oars, certainly the most advanced vessel of the time upon the Mediterranean. Later, Jason and the Argonauts were held to have fled to Corfu for protection from the revenge of Colchis, where they had found the Golden Fleece. Certainly in the epic works of Greek mythology, Corfu was a legendary place, already known for its culture and its sea power, which may have derived from being a trading colony of Phoenician Lebanon or of Minoan Crete.

The maritime emblem of Corfu, from a drawing of a plaque on the facade of the building on Capodistriou Street in which Lord Guilford was converted to the Greek Orthodox Faith.

No trace has yet been found of Ulysses on the beach of Ermones, nor indeed in Ithaca. But the tradition of the past informs the present. We are the heirs of myth, and legends may have elements of truth. What is certain is that the Corinthians, led according to Strabo by a certain Chersicrates, founded the ancient city of Corcyra, embellishing the early ditches and walls at Kanoni. This was one of the early urban civilisations, which enhanced previous attempts at a port and a city. Temples were built in stone, houses lined the avenues, and moles were constructed to shield ships from storms. These were the basic structures of the new sea powers of the Mediterranean, the harbours that could protect the merchantmen and warships of the founders.

Rather as the human body rejects transplants, colonies reject parents. Thucydides recorded that the first naval battle on record was between the Corcyreans, the people of Corfu, and the Corinthians. Very probably the colonists won, because the Corcyreans were in the forefront of naval architecture. They had developed with the tyrants of Greek Sicily, who were also renegade colonists, the fighting boat of the Mediterranean future - the trireme. Briefly Sicily and Corcyra commanded the inland sea with their fifty-oared aggressive weapons that would ram and sink the opposition at a fast stroke: these Greek colonies aided each other against a counter-attack. The mothering cities of Hellas, particularly Corinth and Athens, were briefly backward in naval technology. Although the Corinthians destroyed the independence of Corfu under the tyrant Periander in about 600 BC, the islanders regained their liberty and minted their own coins for commerce after his death. Their pottery distinguished itself from Corinthian ware: they had their own style. And their athletes did well in the Olympic Games.

When Hellas was attacked by a Persian army that crossed the Hellespont, Corfu sent sixty ships to the aid of Athens, although they arrived, owing to the winds, too late to participate in the great battle of Salamis. When the statesman and organiser of victory Themistocles was banished by the envious Athenians, he took refuge on Corfu. And the inhabitants recognised his past wisdom in their dispute with Corinth over the sovereignty of the island of Lefkas: they gave him sanctuary for a time. Bonds were being formed with Athens, the obligations of honour and the past. And these would lead to the alliances that would split Greece asunder in a future fratricidal war.

The thirty years' struggle for supremacy between Athens and Sparta is the subject of the first work of history that can be called impartial, that of Thucydides. When he himself appears in the text, it is in a sentence or two, stating that the Athenians elected him as a general in an expedition against Thrace, that he failed in his manoeuvre and was not asked again to command. Such a sense of proportion and such a refusal of self-justification makes Thucydides the master of Greek history. And as he affirms that the Peloponnesian War was begun in a colony of the Corcyreans, the city of Epidamnos, now called Durrës (Durazzo in Italian), on the

Albanian coast, he makes clear the importance of Corfu as a sea power at the time, with its navy of one hundred and twenty triremes.

A democratic revolution took over Epidamnos; the expelled aristocrats became pirates and attacked their old home. The democrats appealed for help to their mother city in the temple of Hera in Corcyra. That help was refused, so the ambassadors went to Delphi to ask the oracle whether they should hand over their city to Corinthian control. The answer of the gods was yes, and the Corinthians sent a force there. The Corcyreans were furious, and sent a fleet to recapture their colony and put the exiled aristocrats back in power. The Corinthians riposted by sending out their own fleet, which was decisively defeated by the superior Corcyrean triremes. A victory trophy was erected on the headland of Lefkimmi in Corfu. The island navy controlled the southern Adriatic and sacked Corinthian colonies at disputed Lefkas and Kyllene. For the moment, Corfu was dominant in its waters.

Meanwhile Corinth was building a new fleet and the Corcyreans began to be frightened of retaliation. On the old principle of seeking the enemy of an enemy as a friend, they sent ambassadors to Athens to suggest that they should join the Athenian alliance. "We used to think our neutrality was a wise thing," their envoys said, "since it stopped us from being dragged into danger by other people's policies." But now it was a source of weakness, faced with a potential attack by Corinth and its allies. After Athens, Corfu was the greatest naval power in Greece. Together, the two would be invincible and deter any attack from Corinth and indeed from Sparta, which was becoming more and more jealous of rising Athenian power. But if Corinth seized the Corcyrean fleet and combined its ships with her own new navy, then Athens would suffer.

Although Corinth warned Athens that an alliance with its disloyal island colony would lead to outright war, the Athenians felt that the strategic chance was too good to miss and ordered ten ships to help the Corcyreans in a defensive alliance. Unfortunately, the Corinthians and their allies sent a hundred and fifty ships to attack the full rival navy, and the Athenian squadron was drawn into the confused battle, which was more like a combat on land, with interlocked boats grappled together and with hoplites and sailors and archers fighting hand to hand on the decks. Inevitably, Athenians killed Corinthians and were killed by them.

In numbers of ships, it was the biggest encounter yet between two Greek powers. The opportune arrival of a further twenty Athenian ships resulted in a stand-off and a withdrawal by the Corinthian fleet. Although the Corcyreans remained independent - as Thucydides declared - this setback gave Corinth her first cause for war against Athens, because her rival city had fought against her with the Corcyreans, although a peace treaty embracing all the Greek states was in being. This had been broken, Corinth appealed to Sparta for help, and the long war that would enfeeble the old city-states of Hellas would begin, because of the sea power of Corfu.

The Peloponnesian War was not only a struggle for external trade and command of the seas, but also an internal conflict between democrats and aristocrats and tyrants for control of the various cities and states, as had been shown at Epidamnos. Again, Corfu was an instigator and microcosm of political conflict; Thucydides devotes a whole chapter to the revolution there, saying that the islanders were "the first to display in their city the passions of civil war". The Corcyrean prisoners taken by Corinth in their attack on Epidamnos had been well treated in order to act as a fifth column on their return to Corfu and bring the island round to the support of oligarchic Corinth and Sparta rather than democratic Athens. The aristocrats put the leader of the democrats, Peithias, on trial on the charge of making Corfu the slave of Athens. He retaliated by accusing five of his wealthiest opponents of cutting props for their vines on the ground sacred to Zeus and King Alcinous. Huge fines were assessed, an appeal was made and refused. The enraged aristocrats burst upon the democratic council and Peithias, and they killed sixty of their enemies. The few who escaped took refuge on an Athenian trireme in the harbour.

Civil war now broke out in the city of Corcyra, with the democrats helped by their women hurling down tiles from the roofs. The aristocrats fired their arsenal and set nearly all the houses ablaze. Athenian ships now arrived, followed by Corinthian and Spartan vessels, each ready to help their supporters. An inconclusive sea fight was resolved by the arrival of sixty more ships from Athens, which led to a slaughter of the aristocrats. "There was death in every shape and form," Thucydides wrote. "People went to every extreme. Fathers killed their own sons, men were dragged from the temples of the gods and killed on the altars. Some were walled up in the Temple of Dionysus and starved to death there."

The revolution was running out of control, and yet it was the prototype of a hundred urban civil riots during the long conflict between Athens and Sparta. "It became a natural thing for anyone who wanted a change of government to call in help from outside." Corfu's tragedy was to give up its policy of strict neutrality. It began to lose its independence as the other Greek city states did, allying themselves to one major power or the other. "Revenge was more important than self-preservation," Thucydides noted. "Family relations were a weaker bond than party membership." A victory won by treachery was a sign of superior intelligence. But all these massacres and turmoils were caused by the love of power, operating through greed and personal ambition. The moderates were destroyed by the extremists, simplicity by guile. "There was a general deterioration of character throughout the Greek world." Society was divided into two hostile ideologies. No guarantee or oath could be trusted. Only survival mattered. And in Corcyra occurred the preliminary breakdown of law and order, the beginning of chaos.

When the Athenian fleet sailed away, the surviving aristocrats established a base on the mainland and raided across the straits. Then they took over the north of the island, establishing a base on Mount Istone, now called Pantokrator. Although they were initially successful in a guerrilla war, the arrival of a large Athenian force on its way to Sicily led to an attack on the aristocrats in their mountain stronghold and their surrender. The prisoners were put on the small island of Ptychia and then deceived into trying to escape by boat and taken for judgement to Corcyra. There they were penned in a large building, removed in batches to stagger between two lines of hoplites, and so beaten and hacked to death. Those who refused to run the gauntlet

The village of Kassiopi with the mountains of Albania in the distance, shown here in a watercolour by William Page. Private collection.

were killed in the building and their women sold as slaves. So the popular party triumphed by destroying its enemies with the help of the Athenians. "It had been a great revolutionary struggle," Thucydides noted, but now it was over: one of the parties had practically ceased to exist.

From being a focus of the Peloponnesian War, Corfu now became a backwater, although it still saw many upheavals and invasions. Fifteen ships and Corcyrean troops joined in the fatal Athenian expedition to take Syracuse, and they ended sunk or dead or slaves in the Sicilian quarries. The war between the aristocrats and the democrats on the island resumed; again the democrats were helped by an Athenian fleet under Conon: a compromise was stitched over the old wounds. At the end of the Peloponnesian War, Athens cobbled together another confederacy or alliance, and Corfu joined the league again. Attacked by a Spartan force with sixty ships and fifteen hundred hoplites, the Corcyrean fleet was destroyed and the island ravaged, but a counter-attack dispersed the Spartans and a relieving Athenian fleet under the brilliant general Iphicrates drove away the invaders.

The political war had no end, however, and the renegade Athenian general Chares led the aristocrats to bloody victory against their old democratic enemies. The alliance with Athens was renounced, and Corfu regained a kind of independence. Intermittently occupied by the Spartans, Sicilians, Macedonians and Illyrians, it became a pawn in the struggle for supremacy in the Adriatic. Naval technology had moved from the shipyards of Corcyra. Independence was only now possible between the campaigns of greater powers. A long accommodation with the reigning powers now began, particularly when in 229 BC. the Romans took over the strategic island, which was the first Greek city to offer allegiance to Rome.

For five centuries, the Romans governed in Corfu with a tolerant regime. It was their chief harbour and naval base for their long campaigns in Illyria, Epiros, Macedonia and mainland Greece. There was even an attempt by the Macedonians, in alliance with Hannibal and the Carthaginians after his victory at Cannae, to capture Corfu, but it was aborted. It had become and would remain the springboard for the land assault of Western Europe on the East. And although it avoided any more insular civil wars, it could not avoid those of the Roman Empire. It backed the wrong man in the struggle of Pompey against Julius Caesar and became the refuge of his defeated forces after the battle of Pharsalos. Again Mark Antony held the island, but it was captured by Octavian and a Roman fleet before they proceeded to destroy Mark Antony and Cleopatra at the decisive battle of Actium (31 BC). It remained essential in the naval strategy of Western Europe's push towards the Near East.

On a lighter - and probably false - note, the Emperor Nero gave a song recital in 66 AD at Kassiopi. He was notorious for winning all musical contests and even the Olympic Games with his dulcet voice and lyre. As an athlete and actor and singer, he won more than eighteen hundred prizes at festivals and competitions in Greece, where he was often compared to Phoebus Apollo. He believed that this was the praise due to his genius, not to his position. Although he occasionally burned Rome, he thought that the golden laurels should always rest upon his brow. Even when he fell out of his chariot in a race at the Olympics, he was awarded the first place. Eventually condemned by the Senate to be flogged to death by rods, his last words before committing suicide were: "What a loss I am to the arts." It was Corfu's good fortune to have heard him sing once.

*The two Byzantine icons of
St. Jason and St. Sosipatros which
are kept in the 10th-century church
of the same name.*

*Opposite page.
The church of St. Jason and
St. Sosipatros represents the only
Byzantine monument of this type
on the island.*

There are few Greek and Roman remains in modern Kerkyra outside the Archaeological Museum. It is more a Venetian fortress city than a Roman one, although its strength and beauty still attest to its importance as the stepping-stone to the Near East and the keystone of the Adriatic. The mask of Medusa in the museum is exceptional, and there are surviving inscriptions to the Emperors Antoninus Pius, Germanicus and Septimius Severus. Kassiopi was developed into a major port, and to this day its public buildings stand on Roman foundations. Cicero spent a week there, and it is mentioned by Strabo and Ptolemy, Suetonius and Pliny the Elder.

The coming of Christianity to the island in 70 AD through the preaching of the Saints Jason and Sosipatros, associates of Saint Paul, is commemorated in the Byzantine church at Garitsa, also built on classical foundations. With the conversion of the Emperor Constantine to Christianity and the removal of the imperial capital from Rome to Constantinople, Corfu's importance as a maritime base between Italy and Greece and Asia Minor became more evident to the great Church Council at Nicaea in 325 AD. The Corcyrean Bishop Apollodorus was sent and there met the future patron saint of the island, Bishop Spyridon of Trimython in Cyprus.

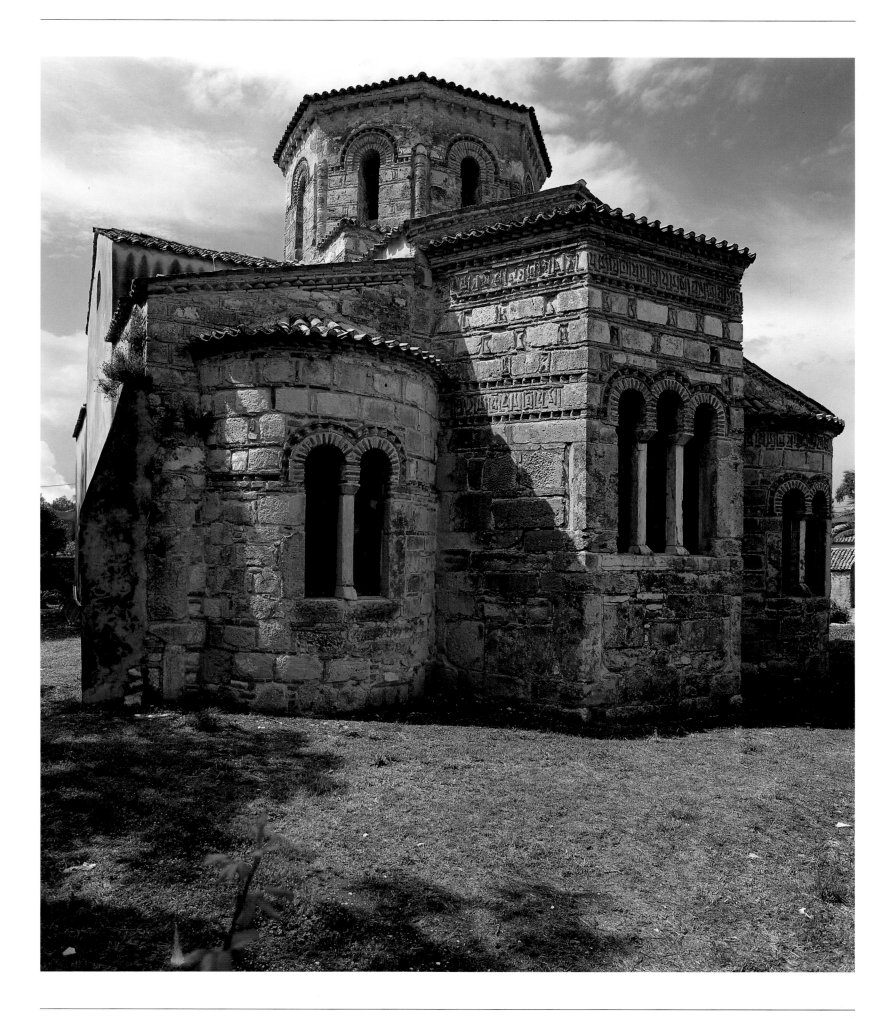

Greek was the language of the church, not Latin, and the home of Orthodox Christianity was now considered to be in Constantinople, and not Rome.

A silver icon of St. Spyridon,
the Patron Saint of Corfu.
Private collection.

With the break-up of the Roman Empire, Corfu was ravaged by successive barbarian invaders. The Huns, Vandals and Goths raided and plundered. In the counter-attack of the Byzantine general Belisarius under the Emperor Justinian, the Corcyreans helped his reconquest of Southern Italy, as they did the Emperor Heraclius in his defeat of King Chosroes II of Persia, and the Emperor Leo the Isaurian in his defence of Constantinople against the Saracens. But the island had paid a heavy price for its strategic importance: the whole of ancient Corcyra was

burned to the ground, its population was massacred by the Goths and the new mediaeval city was built two kilometres to the north on the natural fort of the double-peaked rock called Korypho (or summit) on the peninsula beside the harbour of Alcinous, now named Garitsa Bay. This new port was placed by Leo the Isaurian under the ecclesiastical authority of the Patriarch of Constantinople, and the island was designated a *theme* under the control of a *strategos* or general, who could defend the people from the Saracens and other pirates in return for their support in imperial campaigns in Illyria. Famous for its wine and olives and salt-pans as well as its shipbuilding, Corfu entered on a period of prosperity. Yet it was again doomed by its position to fall into the abyss of the schism between the Greek and Roman Church. The Normans, who had invaded the Mediterranean from the Viking northlands, took Sicily and Southern Italy, where they accepted the papal suzerainty of Rome. In 1081, Robert Guiscard, a formidable Norman warrior, occupied Corfu and held the island against a counter-attack by Byzantine and Venetian forces. Guiscard used this base to besiege Durazzo as a preliminary for marching on Constantinople, but his death sent him to eternity rather than the Hellespont. Dante even placed him in the fifth sphere of paradise. His was the first riposte of the Roman rite against the Greek Orthodox faith, which would culminate in the Fourth Crusade.

The son of Robert Guiscard, Bohemond, briefly held the island, but he was displaced by the Byzantines, who lost control again to the Normans led by King Roger II of Sicily. In 1148 AD, the brother-in-law of the Emperor Manuel Comnenos besieged the walled Norman city with a Venetian fleet, and was killed in the attempt. The citadel was surrendered the following year, and Corfu returned to Byzantine control except for another brief period of Norman occupation forty years later. And from the great harbour of Corcyra, the treacherous fleet of the Fourth Crusade sailed, to take not Jerusalem but Constantinople, and return it to Venetian and Frankish rule. "Never had such a beautiful sight been seen," wrote Geoffrey de Villehardouin, the French chronicler of the Crusade. "And it really did look like a fleet that was to conquer the world, because as far as the eye could see there were only sails of small and big craft, so that men's hearts were full of rejoicing."

The Emperor Manuel Comnenos from the Marmora family history book.

The famous "Gorgon", one of the few well preserved ancient remains, is the oldest stone pediment of this size in Greece. It is housed in the Archeological Museum, Corfu.

The price asked by the Venetians for ferrying the crusaders to Constantinople and the wrecking of the Byzantine empire was the imperial possessions in the Adriatic, including Corfu. It fell into Venetian hands for nine years, in spite of an attempt on it by a Genoese corsair. It was divided among ten Venetian feudal lords, who were charged with defending the island; but they failed when they were assaulted by the Despots of Epiros, a house of bastard Byzantine princes on the Greek mainland. Curiously enough, a previous King of Epiros, the famous Pyhrrus, had passed through Corfu to attack Rome, only to withdraw after his series of expensive, henceforth, "Pyhrric" victories.

These new despots from Epiros stayed to govern Corfu for fifty years, restoring the supremacy of the Greek Orthodox rite. A fortress and a monastery were built on the hill above Paleokastritsa; the Greek churches were exempted from taxes, and the *pappas* (priests) from forced labour. The island prospered, but was given as part of his daughter's dowry by the Despot Michael II to Manfred, King of the Two Sicilies. When Manfred was routed at the battle of Benevento in 1266 AD, the victorious Charles of Anjou, the King of Naples, took over Corfu, again considering it as the best base for an attack on the rest of Greece.

For a hundred and twenty years, the Angevins held on to Corfu. The Orthodox faith was oppressed, and the Greek Metropolitan of Corfu was deposed in favour of a Catholic Archbishop.

While the Corfiots were also ruled harshly and bled for taxes, the Jews from mainland Greece were encouraged to form a community in Corcyra. The Byzantine *strategos* was replaced by a *Capitano*, who ruled through Italian officials and twenty-four fiefs, many of which belonged to members of the Tocco family. Unfortunately after the Sicilian Vespers of 1282 AD, when the Sicilians massacred all the French on their island, drove out the Angevin dynasty and invited the House of Aragon to rule them, two Spanish and Sicilian fleets raided Corfu at the end of the thirteenth century. So rich a place was always worth the looting.

The Angevins, however, kept control of the strategic island until 1386 AD, when Charles III of Anjou died. The linchpin of the Adriatic, Corfu was bound to be gobbled up again by the warring states of the Mediterranean. And so the people turned to a former occupier, now the greatest maritime power in the region. On 28 May, Admiral Giovanni Miani was given the keys of the fortress city in the church of San Angelo (now called San Francesco). The Lion of St Mark was carved on the walls of the citadel and flew on the flags above the battlements. Venice would rule this jewel and bastion of the Adriatic for more than four hundred years, as long as the Romans had. Independence was out of the question for Corfu. It had to settle for another sea power and become the forward base of a foreign trade empire. Once powerful enough to have been a cause of the Peloponnesian War, it was now merely a forward citadel of Christendom.

4 History

2 The Venetian Rule

Michael Pratt

"Ruler of one quarter and half a quarter of the whole Empire of Romania" was how the Doge of Venice described himself, after the Fourth Crusade had seized Constantinople in 1204 and dismembered the Byzantine Empire. A part of the Venetian share was Corfu, Paxos, and the adjoining islands. On this occasion, the Venetians ruled Corfu for less than a decade. It was not until the late fourteenth century that they regained sovereignty, this time for a period lasting four centuries.

The Corfiots were persuaded to hoist the Banner of St Mark once more by the skilful eloquence of Giovanni Miani, the Captain of the Gulf. By negotiations concluded in 1386 all the traditional privileges were guaranteed, with all fiefs and titles of nobility confirmed. In return the community surrendered its time-honoured exemption from taxes and duties, provided the walls were repaired. The Republic's promise never to dispose of Corfu, and to ensure its defence, was enshrined in the Golden Bull, regarded henceforth as the charter of the island's liberties. Venice's position was formalised in 1402, when Corfu and its dependencies were bought from the Angevins for 30,000 gold ducats.

It was indeed fortunate that the Corfiots were now protected by a great maritime nation, for the rising power of the Ottoman Turks hung like a gigantic stormcloud over Eastern Europe.

Constantinople fell to them in 1453, and their armies occupied Greece a few years later. Some 30,000 refugees poured into the Ionian Islands and, virtually unaided, Venice was forced to fight the strongest military power since Imperial Rome. After sporadic warfare, a precarious peace was patched together whereby the Republic retained six of the seven islands. Releasing these controlled Venetian trade routes to the Levant, the Turks still coveted them, mainly biding their time.

In 1537 Sultan Suleiman the Magnificent found an excuse for an attack, when one of his merchantmen was accidentally sunk by a naval patrol in the Strait of Otranto. Refusing to accept any apologies, he sent an army, 25,000 strong, under Khaireddin Barbarossa, which landed on Corfu in late August. Soon only the Old Fortress and Angelokastro, the impregnable fifteenth-century castle on the island's west coast, remained in Christian hands. Luckily the Old Fortress was well defended by a 4,000-strong garrison, half Greek and half Italian, under Jacopo di Novello, which with 700 guns replied briskly to Barbarossa's heavy bombardment. The state of provisions within the citadel was far less fortunate, and starvation loomed within a week. It was averted only by driving the old men, women and children out of the gates to forage in no-man's-land. But the Turkish victualling was little better, while pestilence raged in their ranks. When several assaults had failed to carry the fortifications, they reluctantly re-embarked.

Nevertheless they had wrought havoc in a siege lasting barely three weeks. Farms, villages and vineyards had been devastated throughout Corfu; over 20,000 captives had been carried off and until about 1600 the island's population remained static, at a mere 17,500. During the entire sixteenth century the Adriatic enjoyed truces, but not an enduring peace, while the Barbary pirates terrorized the coastlines and interrupted commercial traffic every summer.

The lion of Venice,
symbol of Venetian rule in Corfu.

Opposite page.
A brooding study of the fortress.

After the great victory of Lepanto in 1571, where the combined fleets of the Holy League, consisting of Spain, Venice and the Papacy, commanded by Don John of Austria, crushed the Ottoman navy, the position did improve. Corfu had contributed four galleys and 1,500 sailors to the allied fleet; one captain had been captured and flayed alive, but another, Cristofalo Kondokali, took the Turkish flagship, which was exhibited in the Arsenal.

The fortifications were intermittently improved, when money was available, and in 1588 the New Fortress was completed, to protect Corfu on the landward side. Wells were dug, a wall built to the water cisterns, and shelters erected for the population against another full-scale invasion. Yet the town was still not entirely walled, nor had earthworks been constructed on the dominant heights of Mounts Abraham and San Salvator. Moreover the heavy expenditure, over 1,800,000 ducats in Corfu alone, meant a permanent deficit, worsened by peculation on the part of underpaid officials. Bribery and maladministration of justice became commonplace. Attempts to revive agriculture by encouraging farmers to cultivate more land and buy more beasts of burden were only partially successful. Millet was introduced, production from the salt-pans, like the wine and olive oil harvests, was boosted, yet Corfu was still not self-sufficient in food. Unless the situation improved, the Republic could not offer sufficient subsidies, nor lighten the burden of taxation.

Ironically the Corfiots benefited from the increase in piracy, which contributed to the long-term decline of Venice. By 1600 there were many non-Moslem predators in Ionian waters; not only the Protestant seamen of England and Holland, but privateers fitted out by the Spanish viceroys of Naples and Sicily, or by the Knights of St John of Malta as well. Commerce certainly suffered, yet increased naval expenditure, with more timber and provisions needed, more crews to spend money in port and vastly expanded dry dock and caulking facilities, were good for the island. Many Corfiots were anyway quite happy to trade with the newcomers, unanimously loathing the Republic's protectionist policy, which required them to send all their exports through Venice.

By the seventeenth century the balance of power had changed irreversibly and the Republic was no longer a vital factor in European affairs. The final loss to the Turks in 1669, after protracted fighting, of Crete, the jewel of the Venetian empire in the Levant, made Corfu into the vital stronghold, the springboard for any attempt to recapture the lost territories. Most recommendations for strengthening the island's defences were ignored, but the Republic seized its opportunity for revenge in 1683, after the Ottoman repulse from before the walls of Vienna. Francesco Morosini, the Captain-General who had marched out from Candia with the honours of war, was reinstated and sent to command the Ionian Islands. After capturing Lefkas and various neighbouring islands, he invaded the mainland in 1685 with a polyglot army, 9,500 strong. Within three years he had conquered virtually the whole Peloponnese and Athens too-gains that were substantially retained in the subsequent peace treaty.

Unfortunately Venetian rule in Greece proved even less popular than Turkish, and mutual antipathies grew during the fifteen-year occupation. The Republic, aggressively Catholic but militarily weak, presented an easy target once Ottoman fortunes had revived. In 1715 its power on the mainland collapsed in a campaign of just 100 days. Lefkas was again abandoned, and Corfu would obviously be the next target for the Turks. A new Captain-General, Count Johann Matthias von der Schulenburg, was appointed. A Saxon soldier of fortune, whose sister was George I's mistress, he had served with distinction under Marlborough and Charles XII of Sweden. He straightaway embarked for Corfu, repairing the fortifications as time permitted, arming all the citizens and laying in adequate provisions and munitions. Yet his preparations were scarcely completed when on 5 July 1716 the Turkish fleet was sighted.

Just as in 1537, Gouvia was the chosen point of disembarkation; an army of 30,000 infantry and 3,000 cavalry, commanded by Kara Mustapha Pasha, was landed. The town was closely invested by land and sea, but a Venetian relief squadron under Andrea Pisani burst through the enemy's blockade, arriving safely in the harbour with the loss of one ship. Corfu's seaward defences were now formidable. On the landward side, however, despite an array of new bastions, outworks and glacis, which stretched from Garitsa Bay round to Mandouki, the commanding heights of Mounts Abraham and San Salvator had still not been properly fortified.

The statue of the famous mercenary warrior, Count Johann Matthias von der Schulenburg, prominently placed in front of the old fortress.

The full fury of the Ottoman attack was to be concentrated upon them. After the second assault the defenders of Mount Abraham had been overwhelmed, while those on Mount San Salvator had fled. Schulenburg contemptuously rejected the summons to surrender. Yet he wrote: "I am in want of everything"; and his motley garrison of Greeks, Slavs, Italians and Germans barely amounted to 8,000. Kara Mustapha Pasha now turned his attention to the New Fortress. His troops attacked it day after day, and were as regularly repulsed. The garrison even made a dawn sortie, although in the ensuing *mêlée* the Slavs were assailed by the Germans, and some 200 were slain.

On the night of 17 August, the Ottoman general led his entire army into battle. The garrison, everywhere outnumbered, fell back, and the Turks fought their way into the New Fortress. After a fierce six-hour struggle, Schulenburg with 800 men debouched from the Porta Raimonda and took the enemy in flank, driving them back

to their lines with 2,000 dead and twenty standards left behind. His reckless courage had saved Corfu. Nevertheless, another assault seemed imminent, and there was doubt whether the fortifications would hold.

When the fateful morning broke, there was no sign of the Turks. Closer inspection revealed a deserted camp and the army re-embarking. A terrible storm the night before had washed their baggage into the sea. The islanders claimed that a heavenly host, led by their patron Saint Spyridon, had been seen in the sky, and the politic Venetians encouraged this belief in divine intervention. Actually the approach of a Spanish fleet, the murmurs of the unpaid Janissaries and news of a major Turkish defeat on the Danube had been the deciding factors. Ottoman losses after the forty-three-day siege were heavy: 15,000 killed by sword or plague, and another 900 drowned in the hurried embarkation. Schulenburg was suitably honoured by a grateful Republic (his statue still stands on the Spianada, the huge open space in the middle of the town, which today serves, *inter alia,* as the cricket ground). War continued until 1718, when Venice renounced all mainland claims in perpetuity.

The eighteenth century was an age of illusory security for Corfu. True, some problems had disappeared, for Ottoman Turkey had begun its long decline, and the Habsburg alliance had been proclaimed eternal. Venice maintained friendly relations with the semi-independent chieftains in Albania and Epirus; the Barbary pirates were bought off, while the traders from northern Europe were now respectable merchants, not privateers. Yet lawlessness was increasing, and once the outside threats which had united the whole population had passed, the deepening abyss separating the classes became apparent. The townspeople and peasants, whose lot had scarcely improved since the Middle Ages, disliked each other, while many of the latter, having borrowed against their harvests, were irretrievably in debt. If the peasantry disliked its oppressors, the bourgeoisie, growing in wealth and self-confidence, resented the nobility's monopoly of public office and personal prestige.

It was reported in 1724 that there were over 3,000 bandits in the islands, many in areas inaccessible to the authorities. Appeals to them to surrender and expiate their crimes in the Republic's galleys were largely ignored. With arms so readily

An old map of Corfu town as it was in the sixteenth century, showing the fortifications of the fortress and the moat. Gennadeion Library, Athens.

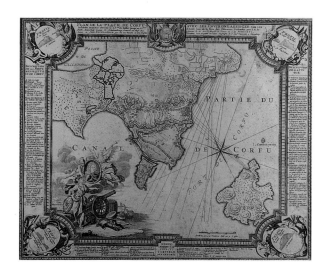

A map of Corfu as it was under Venetian rule. The vignettes framing the map show various castles on the island. Gennadeion Library, Athens.

Opposite page. A typical old belfry and tall Venetian buildings in the heart of Corfu town.

available, most nobles kept a band of hired *bravi*. Brawls and vendettas became habitual; soon there was a graduated tariff for wearing weapons. One English traveller thus described the prevailing anarchy in 1790: "By what I learned, the police are really shocking. The governors are generally needy men, but by accepting fines for remission for murder they are quickly enriched, perhaps by the ruin of the widow and orphans. Is your husband assassinated? Dry up your tears - your governor is three guineas richer. Do you remonstrate? For three guineas you may let loose all the demons of revenge. So one murder produces another; whole families are involved in destruction, or else live in perpetual alarms. Justice never interferes, and society is of course destroyed".

High-cost shipping, low-quality crews and discriminatory tariffs had so debased Venice's commercial status that the Corfiots were perforce tied to a stagnant economy. Likewise they formed part of a political system that had ossified, where a small oligarchy held power and mollified malcontents by handing out a few crumbs of office.

Changed from a productive to a rentier economy, the regime remained stable, served by an efficient and fundamentally lenient bureaucracy. The Ionians could still find a market for their olive oil, or currants from the southern islands, but the free-ranging Renaissance spirit, alert for new ventures, had gone.

One conscientious administrator, the *provveditore generale*, N.H. Grimani, descried impending ruin. In a long memorandum of November 1760, he listed the problems. Over half the oil produced on Corfu was being exported, for only one-seventh was consumed locally, yet customs receipts had slumped. Two more state patrol vessels were urgently needed. He condemned the prevalence of usury, steeply rising prices and restrictive policies, which meant all raw materials and consumer goods had to be imported. If Corfu became a free port, he informed the Senate, it could again become an entrepôt of East-West trade.

Nothing was done of course, and the administration slid further towards impotence and corruption. By the 1780s there was only a meagre garrison on Corfu, scarcely 5,000 men, whose pay was so far in arrears that they had to find private employment to buy provisions. The cannon's mouths were clogged with earth, the ditches with crumbling masonry. The officers carried dead or disbanded men on their lists to line their pockets, while the genuinely ill were put into hospital without pay or food to subsist on public charity. It was the same story with the fleet. Corfu was Venice's naval headquarters for the Levant, with two squadrons, one of twenty-five galleys, the other of twelve heavy sailing ships, each under a Vice-Admiral. They were supposed to undertake one campaign a year in peacetime, being repaired in winter at the Gouvia Arsenal. But activity there was confined to careening and basic maintenance; and the number of ships steadily diminished, with many captains scuttling their unseaworthy vessels, while others went off on commercial cruises.

Before the decadence of their eighteenth-century governments, however, Venetian rule in Corfu had been effective. The first senior official sent out after 1386 had been the bailo, who was in charge of the civilian administration, and soon afterwards the office of *provveditore* was created, to command the fortress and garrison, with the authority to dispense judgement in civil and criminal cases.

From the later sixteenth century a new supremo was appointed; the *Provveditore Generale del Levante*, whose responsibilities extended throughout the Republic's Ionian territories, and who commanded the fleet as well. A great nobleman, appointed directly by the Grand Council for a three year term, his arrival and investiture were scenes of solemn ceremony, regulated by exact etiquette. Triumphal arches were erected, fireworks and musical tableaux organised, while the festivities often lasted for several days. The island's dignitaries greeted him on landing, the large Jewish community provided carpets for the streets, both the Catholic and Orthodox clergy held splendid services. The procession wound its way round the town until reaching the Church of St Spyridon, where the *Provveditore Generale* knelt before the saint's relics and swore to respect the Corfiots' customs.

By 1700 his staff had grown to include a secretary, an interpreter for Oriental languages and a treasurer, all appointed from Venice, while he chose his own Chancellor for legal matters, *aides-de-camp* and military inspectors.

Considerable state was kept in his palace within the Old Fortress; four liveried servants were employed with two messengers, who played the horn and trumpet alternately during meals. Receptions and banquets had to be given for all sections of the community, with the guest lists strictly prescribed. In theory, the *Provveditore Generale*, whose expenses invariably exceeded his salary, was rich and high-minded enough to remain a disinterested public servant. In reality, most appointees hired their plate, liveries and furniture from the Jews, whose charges, in return for services rendered, they sometimes forgot to repay.

By the eighteenth century, corruption had become institutionalised. At the five formal banquets given every year, always excellent meals, the guest was supposed to slip under his plate a promissory note for so many measures of oil, payable in cash or kind after the first harvest. An ADC collected the slips and showed them to his chief, who modulated the warmth of his farewells accordingly. Similarly every New Year all citizens had to throw a coin into the boxes by the palace gates, while officials requesting gifts sat at small tables along the corridors. The next day a drummer with two soldiers was sent round to the richer inhabitants to remind them that their security and generosity were indivisible. Holes in the shape of lions' mouths were strategically placed in walls around the town, in which anonymous denunciations could be placed. Those denounced were brought before the Chancellor to deposit a caution, which they never dared reclaim.

In 1386 a Council composed entirely of nobles had been formed to represent the Corfiots' interests. By 1490 its number had risen to 150, which was to remain constant. A variety of local officials were elected from its ranks, including the three annual judges, four *sindaci*, the clerk of the court, two assessors of legal costs, weights and measures inspectors, three poor relief fund administrators, three health intendants and three country magistrates. The prestige attaching to the Trierarch, who commanded the war galleys, was enormous. There was unfailingly fierce competition for all offices, however honorific or unprofitable, and political intrigue abounded at Council meetings. But the Council's functions became gradually nominal, as an inner conclave of twelve officials held its sessions behind closed doors.

The nobles' names were inscribed in the *Libro d'Oro* as a permanent record. After the 1537 siege Venice ensured that its ranks were refilled from the middle classes; there were 112 families listed in 1672, but 277 by 1797, for by then the impoverished Republic had long been selling patents of nobility to any rich citizen. The system eventually degenerated into farce. Theoretically disbarred from engaging in trade, jewellers and chemists were deemed adequately dignified professions, while naturally lawyers proliferated.

By the eighteenth century the aristocracy still monopolised the municipal administration, but its functions were increasingly futile, for the *sindaci* had no money with which to compensate suppliants, while the health inspectors' quarantine was disregarded in Italian ports.

The peasantry seldom complained on Corfu, and for the first several centuries Venetian rule had been reasonably beneficial. The government gave twelve gold pieces for every hundred olive trees planted, so that slowly they covered the island. Even if export duties were high - 15 per cent on oil, 9 on salt, and 4 on everything else - agriculture remained quite healthy. Only by the eighteenth century did wheat and maize, the peasants' staple diet, have to be imported, while there remained plenty of fish, fruit and vegetables. By then wine too was imported; hitherto a successful industry, the vintages had become thick and sweet, and did not keep.

One of Venice's most successful ways of retaining Corfiot loyalties was its skilful handling of the Orthodox Church. Less bigoted than most Catholic powers, it preserved a balance between Pope and Patriarch, for though the Archbishop was an Italian, the Corfiots had their own chief priest, chosen by "the Sacred Band" of thirty-two town priests. Though simony was more important than sanctity, the clergy were still popular, while the Republic thwarted any attempt from Rome to tamper with Orthodox services. Inter-denominational relations were good, with mixed marriages permitted, communal services, and everyone joining in the great religious processions. The Republic astutely fostered the cult of St Spyridon, Corfu's patron saint, who enjoyed four splendid festivals a year. The local good will thus engendered counterbalanced the Venetian failure to provide education for the islanders, but it could not ultimately save the regime.

The final act was to begin in 1794. The last *Provveditore Generale,* Carlo Aurelio Widmann, arrived that July with the best of intentions and the worst of illusions. He found the treasury empty, with a visible trade deficit of 100,000 ducats, an unpaid garrison and just four ships left in the entire Levant fleet. He boldly appealed to public generosity and achieved much, although he got no help from Venice. In 1796 the Republic, contemplating war with France, decided to defend Corfu, ignoring its own insolvency and the ruinous fortifications. Furthermore, the Levant fleet was summoned back to defend the Lagoon. Well might Widmann write, as 1797 dawned: "I am on the brink of a catastrophe."

Not more than half the year had passed before this prophecy was fulfilled, with the ending of four centuries of Venetian rule. It had brought much good as well as latterly some bad to the island. Many Corfiots had reason to lament with Wordsworth the Republic's fall:

"Once did She hold the gorgeous east in fee,
And was the safeguard of the west: the worth
Of Venice did not fall below her birth,
Venice, the eldest Child of Liberty".

"The Liston" where once only the noble families inscribed in the Libro d'Oro could promenade.

Count John Capodistrias, First President of independent Greece.

Opposite page.
John Capodistrias's desk, preserved in the library of the Reading Society.

On 8 May 1797, following Napoleon Bonaparte's brilliant campaign in Northern Italy, the Venetian Senate signified its readiness to accept the conqueror's terms. La Serenissima had politically ceased to exist and its empire lay open to the first taker. Napoleon was in no doubt who that should be. He always considered, to the point of obsession, that the Ionian Islands, Corfu principal among them, were the key to the Eastern Mediterranean and thus to the route to the Orient. Accordingly he hastened to take possession of Corfu and the other islands, employing the artful ruse of combining a French fleet with a Venetian convoy, the ships sailing under the Venetian flag.

When the fleet arrived at the end of June 1797 French troops, under the command of the Corsican general Gentili, were initially well received. Most of the population welcomed the promise of new liberties and an end to the power of the aristocracy. These feelings did not last very long. The newcomers caused much offence by appointing two Jews to the Municipal Council, as well as by their disrespectful attitude towards religion, which included - horror of horrors - the mocking of St Spyridon.

Yet this first French occupation, formalised by the Treaty of Campo Formio's transfer of sovereignty to France, brought some tangible benefits. In May 1798 the French installed in Corfu the first printing press to be known in Greece. They also abolished the feudal system, burnt the *Libro d'Oro*, laid down plans for improved education and substituted Greek for Italian as the official language (though this last edict had no practical effect until much later).

But none of this was enough to win the co-operation of the islanders, who soon discovered that these revolutionary French were just as penniless, and just as inclined to impose taxes, as the Venetians. When therefore Russia and Turkey

joined the second coalition against France, and dispatched a combined fleet to reconquer the islands, their troops found in some of them a ready welcome. Corfu, with its French garrison, proved a tougher nut to crack. Only after several months' siege and some fierce engagements did the French commander Chabot admit himself beaten. When Russian troops entered Corfu town in March 1799, they were enthusiastically greeted and the church bells pealed. The tactful Russian commander, Admiral Ushakov, proceeded immediately to St Spyridon's church, there to give thanks for the victory.

For the next seven years, the seven islands enjoyed the status of an independent federal state - the Septinsular Republic - under the protection of Russia but paying tribute to Constantinople. It was a curious and unnatural arrangement. If the Ionians saw in the Tsar the protector of their Orthodox faith, they regarded the Turkish part of the condominium with deep revulsion. At least after 1801 they did not have to endure the physical presence of either Turks or Russians, who withdrew their troops. But in response to continuous disorders, amounting almost to anarchy, Russian forces were soon back, this time accompanied as Russian plenipotentiary by Count Mocenigo, a Venetian born in Zakinthos and trained in the Imperial service in St Petersburg. Neither his skills nor those of the Corfiot Count John Capodistrias (later to become the first President of independent Greece) could devise a constitution acceptable to the quarrelsome Ionian factions. By 1807, the Franco-Russian Treaty of Tilsit had restored the islands to French rule.

This second French occupation (1807-14) was marked first by the wise and humane rule of Governor-General Donzelot (one of the main streets in Corfu town, bordering the harbour, is called after him), and second by the conquest of the southern Ionian Islands by the British and by

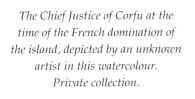

their not very energetic blockade of Corfu. The executive powers were administered by the French Governor-General and the Senate, which in 1807 appointed a government limited to three ministries: Finance (Count Sordinas); Home Affairs (Count Flamburiari); Justice and Public Order (Count Karatzias). Donzelot remained firmly in control of the islands, and by his reforms and efficient administration made France as popular as before she had been unpopular. This time not only was St Spyridon not ridiculed, but his processions were carried out with proper respect and splendour. Newspapers were published, the Ionian Academy for the Encouragement of the Arts and Sciences founded, agriculture improved, and the whole system of government, still based upon mediaeval Venetian laws, overhauled. Under the direction of Mathieu de Lesseps (father of the future creator of the Suez Canal), work began on building, on the north side of the Spianada, the handsome houses rising above arcades which recall the Rue de Rivoli in Paris.

Napoleon's abdication in 1814 was followed by a tightening of the British blockade. Donzelot held out until the receipt of an order from the restored Louis XVIII to give way, and on 21 June Corfu came under the control of British troops. Sir James Campbell, Commissioner on behalf of the Allies, immediately closed down the printing presses and the Ionian Academy. There followed some protracted discussions about what to do with the Septinsular Republic. Finally, in November 1815, a treaty was signed in Paris under which the seven islands were defined as constituting "a single, free and independent state under the exclusive protection of His Britannic Majesty". Capodistrias, by now a trusted member of the Tsar's diplomatic service, fought hard for real protectorate status, but despite the treaty's reference to independence, the Ionians were destined to live, for better or for worse, through nearly fifty years of *de facto* rule by Britain.

The treaty specified the appointment of a Lord High Commissioner who should introduce a new constitution. The first holder of the post was Sir Thomas Maitland, the Governor of Malta. The second son of Lord Lauderdale, Maitland was an experienced pro-consul with little or no time for democracy or self-government. "Least of all can I think with temper," he wrote, even before taking up his appointment, "of anything like a

representative government; all that we can do is to correct the abuses that may exist." Although he made use of the local nobility to support his political formulae, he privately despised them. For him the "people" were either illiterate peasants or aristocrats "whose only object is the possession of power for corrupt ends".

Maitland, popularly known as "King Tom" because of his autocratic ways, was a sound administrator, with a clear idea of his objectives and how to achieve them. But his was not an attractive personality. A British contemporary account describes him as "insufferably rude and abrupt, particularly dirty in his person, constantly drunk and surrounded by sycophants". Another writer refers to his language, which "surprised the elegant Ionians by its coarseness".

He installed a Legislative Assembly of forty members, elected on an extremely limited franchise, and a Senate of five. But while these arrangements bore some semblance of parliamentary government, all executive power remained in Maitland's hands, as he had always intended it should. No legislation could take effect without his consent, and he appointed the Residents - all Englishmen - of the other islands, who in their turn could override the authority of local bodies. A supreme Council of Justice, with

four judges - two English, two Greek - was established, and so as to put an end to the corruption of Venetian times, they were paid handsomely.

Mindful of the importance that the Ionians attached to titles and orders, Maitland instituted the Order of St Michael and St George, whose honours were to be bestowed on suitable recipients in the Ionian Islands and Malta.

To equip the new Order with headquarters, as well as to house the Senate and provide a home for the "Lord High", Maitland commissioned the palace that still graces the northern end of the Spianada. Constructed of Maltese sandstone, in neo-classical style with a Doric colonnade, it is an imposing building both inside and out, a fitting monument to Maitland's sense of empire.

His other great legacy to Corfu and the islands was to put their finances on a sound footing, so that money was forthcoming to build new roads and repair churches and public buildings. When he died and was buried in Malta in 1824, he was, despite his uncouth ways, genuinely mourned; special requiem ceremonies were held in Corfu, and some years later a memorial, in the shape of an attractive stone rotunda with Ionic columns, was erected on the upper Spianada by Ionian well-wishers.

The villa of Mon Repos where Prince Philip, The Duke of Edinburgh, was born in 1921.

But great though the material benefits were that King Tom had brought to the islands, the Ionians could not help noting that the British Protectorate had stopped well short of self-government. Returning to Corfu in 1819, Capodistrias became aware of the depth of anti-British feeling.

A German visitor to Corfu in 1821 remarked on a pro-Turkish bias among the local British. This was partly mitigated by Maitland's successor, Sir Frederick Adam, a good-looking, cultivated man, who had already served in Corfu as commander of the garrison. He moved easily among the local aristocratic families, into one of which he married. He and his wife created a sparkling Anglo-Corfiot circle. Private Wheeler, an infantry soldier serving in one of the garrison's battalions, who wrote a number of lively and descriptive letters which have been preserved and published, dubbed Lady Adam, neé Palatianos, "Queen of the Ionian Islands". He was less complimentary about her looks, describing her as having "a beard on her upper lip which would ornament a Huzzar".

Adam served the island well by building roads and particularly, in Corfu, constructing an aqueduct to bring fresh water from Benitses to the town, a distance of some 8 kilometres. Despite the fact that he did not deviate from Maitland's despotic methods of government, he was popular, at least with the aristocracy. Wheeler describes the celebrations which marked his appointment, when "a high holiday took place, much powder was wasted ... the Greeks sang and danced [their slippers] to pieces". Unfortunately, Adam was extravagant and left the Treasury bare. Napier, the gifted and observant Resident in Cephalonia, recorded that the Greeks said of Adam that "while Corfu kept the Lord High Commissioner, Cephalonia paid his tailor and Zante [Zakinthos] his coachmaker". Nevertheless, when he left Corfu in 1832 to become Governor of Madras, the Senate voted funds for his statue in bronze, which stands in front of the Palace - Sir Frederick, dressed in Roman robes, surveying the Spianada.

Another reminder of Adam is the villa of Mon Repos, a few miles to the south of the town, which he had built as a country retreat. Later it became the Greek royal family's summer home, where Prince Philip was born in 1921.

Adam was succeeded by Lord Nugent (1832-5), a politician of a liberal and reforming nature, who was able to make minor adjustments to the Maitland system. But as the cabinet in London remained opposed to any constitutional changes, there was nothing of significance that Nugent could do, and even he was alarmed by the unrest that his mild reforms occasioned. For the political climate was changing.

In 1832, the year of Nugent's appointment, Prince Otto of Bavaria accepted the throne of the newly created Hellenic state. From then on, the desire of the Ionians to be united with their compatriots on the mainland was a permanent

Old Venetian and neo-classical mansions in the Mourayia area.

View of the fortress with the Douglas Obelisk in the foreground, painted by Franz Pige in the nineteenth century.
(oil 47 x 67 cm).
Koutlides collection, Athens.

feature of the political landscape and a permanent point of contention with their British rulers. Even the old aristocracy became resentful at the curtailment of their privileges.

Nugent's successor, General Sir Howard Douglas (1835-41), was more of the Maitland type. Though a good administrator, he was not one to hearken to the voices demanding constitutional change, and was soon at odds with the liberal opposition in the islands. He had to dissolve one Assembly, and proceeded blatantly to back its successor. Yet he had his enlightened moments. He required his staff to learn modern Greek, and was sufficiently objective to write, in a dispatch to London, that "the internal state of the country, the moral and physical state of the people have not been benefited by the British connexion so far as to protect us hereafter from the reproach of having attended less to their interests than to our own". He also, in 1839, helped to create the Ionian Bank, the Greek part of which is now incorporated with the Ionian and Popular Bank of Greece. A memorial column stands today on the road from the town to the airport, with Douglas' achievements inscribed on it. They include the creation of the lunatic asylum and the main prison, both of them still functioning.

After Douglas came Stewart Mackenzie, a liberal whose only memorable achievement was to ensure that revenue exceeded expenditure. He was succeeded by Lord Seaton, a former Governor-General of Canada. Although a Conservative by party, he did much to encourage local government, appointed for the first time an Ionian as Treasurer-General, and then, responding to the upheavals which all over Europe marked the revolutionary year of 1848, proceeded to break with the Maitland system by recommending a new constitution of startlingly liberal flavour, combined with press freedom. The curious situation then ensued of a Whig government in London warning a Conservative High Commissioner not to go so fast, with the latter remaining resolute and, in the end, carrying the day. The Assembly adopted the reforms, with the result, as one observer put it, that "on May 1st, 1849, the Lord High Commissioner had more power than Queen Elizabeth, on the tenth of the same month he was left with less power than Queen Victoria".

Far from quieting the demands for union with Greece, the new reforms, especially that permitting freedom of the press, had the reverse effect. Lord Kirkwall, who served on the staff of

A procession of St. Spyridon in the
old town. Watercolour by Joseph
Cartwright (38 x 63 cm).
Private collection.

the Lord High Commissioner in the early 1850s, wrote that Seaton "did not perceive that the great mass of Ionians cared little for reform, and desired only Union". Seaton's successor, Sir Henry Ward (1849-55), was in a constant struggle with the Assembly, described by Kirkwall as "animated solely by hatred of the British Protectorate and of the local government". More than once, Ward had to prorogue it. He had also to deal with an uprising in Cephalonia, always the most fractious of the islands, which led to martial law, the execution of twenty-one activists, and an increase of anti-British feeling.

Ward's place was taken by Sir John Young, a man generally described as mild and gentle. But these qualities did not save him from the bitter opposition of the Assembly, which became less manageable than ever, having frequently to be prorogued. A dispute between Young and the Municipality of Corfu culminated in an incident during one of St Spyridon's processions. Those processing were accustomed to halt in front of the Palace and offer up a prayer for Queen Victoria. On 23 August 1858 the municipal representatives absented themselves from this ceremony, an action they sought to justify by claiming that Young, on the balcony of the Palace, had failed in the normal courtesies to the saint by not having his uniformed staff with him. The excuse was feeble but the incident served to show the state of tension between the

Protectorate government and the Unionist wing of Ionian politics. That tension was increased further when it became known that Young was recommending the annexation of Corfu and Paxos, which would have become straightforward British colonies, while the southern islands would be ceded to Greece. There was something to be said for the idea, for not only did the other islands lack any strategic importance but Unionist pressures there were much greater than in Corfu itself. Indeed, some Corfiot politicians, such as Curcumelli, actually supported the annexation scheme.

By this time (late 1858) the government in London had decided to send William Gladstone, then in opposition, to the Protectorate to inquire into the obstacles to good government in the islands. A dispatch from the Colonial Office predicted: "His renown as a Homeric scholar will commend him to the sympathies of an Hellenic race." These high expectations were not fulfilled. The Ionians assumed that Gladstone had come to implement the annexation-cession proposals, so that although the great man told the Senate that he was not there to vary the terms of the treaty, everywhere he went he was greeted with Unionist fervour. He visited nearly all the islands (inadvertently banging his head against the chin of the Bishop of Paxos when kissing the latter's episcopal ring), went to Athens, where he was received by the King and Queen, and finally, in

Opposite page.
The belfry of the church of
St. Spyridon as it stands today.

January 1859, recommended the recall of the hapless Young, to be replaced by none other than Gladstone himself.

His rule lasted no more than a fortnight, during which the Assembly passed one resolution for the union of all the islands with Greece, and another rejecting Gladstone's proposals for constitutional reform under the Protectorate. The future Prime Minister, who for all his Philhellene sentiments seemed unable to grasp the simple fact that the majority of the islanders preferred union with Greece to British-sponsored political reforms, resigned his post and returned to England to safeguard his parliamentary constituency.

The last Lord High Commissioner was General Sir Henry Storks (1859-64), an able autocrat who like his predecessor found himself at permanent loggerheads with a recalcitrant Assembly which he had frequently to prorogue. One of the Assembly's suggestions was that he should address it in Greek. As Kirkwall pointed out, the members of the Assembly were perfectly aware that "His Excellency could as easily have addressed them in Chinese or Hebrew."

A way out of the impasse opened up when in 1862 a *coup d'état* in Athens deposed the unpopular King Otto. Greece would have liked to have a British Prince as a sovereign: a national plebiscite opted almost unanimously for Prince Alfred, Duke of Edinburgh, Queen Victoria's second son. But this choice was internationally unacceptable, and in the end, and with British assistance, the Danish Prince William of Glücksberg became King George I of the Hellenes.

As the government in London had previously declared that it would be ready to end its Ionian Protectorate provided a suitable constitutional monarch were installed in Athens, the way was now clear for a new initiative. That consisted of nothing less than a complete and voluntary British withdrawal, a unique occurrence in the history of nineteenth-century empires. Unfortunately the good will this should have generated was quickly dispelled. The original guarantors of the 1815 Treaty of Paris insisted that the seven islands should be neutralised. This required the destruction of most of the fortifications in Corfu, leaving only the Old Fortress and part of the New Fortress. The work of demolition began in

February 1864, to the annoyance and chagrin of the Corfiots, who were proud of this great mass of military architecture, and whose taxes had paid for much of it. In a blaze of misplaced ill-will, scarcely mitigated by a fulsomely - worded farewell address from the Municipal Council, British troops, British officialdom and the Lord High Commissioner himself sailed away on 2 June 1864. Four days later, King George arrived from Athens and immediately repaired to St Spyridon church for a solemn Te Deum.

Summing up the historical event in *The Times*, the editorial writer concluded: "The Islanders and the Protecting Power have parted on excellent terms. The British flag has been hauled down, not by a victorious enemy, not in ungracious concession to seditious and doleful subjects, but with an air of generosity on one side, and gratitude on the other, seldom found in international transactions." This rosy view cannot be altogether accepted. Whatever *The Times* in London thought, the British Protectorate had not on the whole been a happy experience, either for the governors or the governed.

Personal respect for individual Lord High Commissioners, especially among the upper classes, and even the great material benefits that British rule had brought to the islands, counted in the general context for little compared with the Ionian wish for genuine self-government and then, transcending all else, for union with Greece. But against this rather unpromising background, some more pleasing scenes and personalities stand out.

Prominent among these was Frederick North, fifth Earl of Guilford. He had been Maitland's predecessor as Governor of Ceylon, but his principal ambition was to revive the spirit of ancient Greece. His Philhellenism knew no bounds. As a young man, he had been received into the Orthodox Church, and in 1824 he inaugurated in Corfu the Ionian Academy, effectively the first, and until the foundation of the University of Athens the only, university in Greece. Thus for a time Corfu became the intellectual centre of the Greek-speaking world.

Guilford was generous towards the new institution; much of its library of 21,000 volumes came from his own library. Even though his death in 1827 removed most of the driving force behind the Academy, and meant that its activities

Opposite page.
The Liston, a replica of the
Rue de Rivoli in Paris, designed in
1809 by Matthieu de Lesseps whose
son Ferdinand built the Suez Canal.

were reduced, it continued to play an important part in the educational development of the islands.

Guilford was a genuine eccentric. He liked to wear classical Greek robes, with a gold band around his hair. Napier describes him dining with King Tom in 1819: "he entered the room at the head of twelve men, professors in black, with powdered heads, bandy legs, cocked hats under their short arms and snuff boxes in hand ... all the Greeks would speak Italian, the Italians English, the English French and Italian mixed, and the French all the five languages together... Lord Guilford was very pleasant, addressing each person in a different language, and always in that which the person addressed did not understand." On Guilford's death, the Ionian official gazette recorded that "the youth of Greece [has lost] its most loving father and benefactor."

With a few exceptions, such as Adam and Guilford, the British protectors did not mingle much with the protected, unlike the Venetians who assimilated with their subject peoples. The officials and officers and men of the garrison, and their families, led their own lives, looking upon local customs and ceremonies with a sort of amused condescension. A common criticism concerned the idleness (as British observers saw it) of the Corfiots. Gladstone remarked on it disapprovingly and Professor Ansted, who wrote a long book on the state of the islands in 1863, claimed that "it is not the custom of the Corfiot to work when he can remain idle". Private Wheeler describes at length St Spyridon's procession when, "after the whole of the town had been perambulated and half the sick had received their death stroke from the powerful rays of the sun, the saint is once more stood up by the altar, when the old trade of kissing his boots and dropping money in the dish again begins ..." Wheeler's attitude is certainly very disdainful, so that it is only fair to record that, at least in the early days of the Protectorate, it was the custom for four British colonels to carry the saint's casket on procession days.

A recurrent British visitor was Edward Lear (see chapter 10). He was first in Corfu in April 1848, returning in 1855 to spend the winter. His first impression was that there was "no place in the world so lovely". On his second visit he found the scenery just as entrancing, but the social pressure had become too demanding for him: "a more disorganised fiddle-faddle, Poodly-Pumpkin place never was. At the Palace they are rushing about pauselessly and continuously. I suspect that Lady Young [wife of the Lord High Commissioner] would not be happy in heaven if she could not get up an immense ball, or land or water picnics among the angels... it is sadly frivolous work." He spent another winter there in 1861-2, sketching and completing his *Book of Nonsense,* and in the spring of 1863 was there for the last time under British rule. He seems to have overcome his aversion to social life, remarking: "I never before knew Corfu so agreeable and lively... no end of gigantic swells have been here this winter, Dukes, Earls, Barons and what-nots." This was a reference to the island's popularity as a winter refuge among the British moneyed class. Lear's sketches, watercolours and oils of the Corfu landscape or of groups of peasants among the olive groves are among the most desirable mementoes of a more tranquil way of life than generally prevails today. The only remaining traces of British rule now - apart from neo-classical architecture, the road system and the water supply - are cricket (see chapter 14), old-fashioned ginger beer (*tsin-tsin birra*), and a certain predeliction among the educated classes for British modes and customs, especially the English language.

1864 to the Present

Enosis for the Ionian Islands, union with Greece, robbed them of some of their individual institutions. The Ionian Academy was merged with the University of Athens, the Ionian Orthodox Church with the Greek, while the local aristocracy lost whatever remained of their privileged status. But life continued pleasantly enough in Corfu, enlivened by the comings and goings of such illustrious Corfu lovers as the Empress of Austria and Kaiser Wilhelm II (see chapter 6) Old postcards (still obtainable in newsagents' shops) show early twentieth-century scenes in the neighbourhood of Garitsa Bay which are reminiscent of Edwardian England: nurses pushing enormous English prams, little boys bowling hoops, little girls in pinafores. Guidebooks of the period advised intending visitors that "private lodgings are very primitive and scarcely adapted for foreigners". The island, for all its Greekness, retained, as it does today, a pleasant cosmopolitan flavour deriving from its long history of association with the West.

Opposite page.
St. Spyridon's procession.

In the First World War, while Greece remained neutral, the remnants of the Serb army, defeated by Austro-Bulgarian forces, were evacuated to Corfu, which also became the seat of the Serb government-in-exile. Serb cemeteries on Vido Island and elsewhere bear witness to this sombre episode. In 1923, Mussolini, newly installed in power in Rome, ordered a naval bombardment of the island, followed by military occupation. This was in response to the murder on the mainland of the Italian general commanding the international Albanian boundary commission.* There was no proof that Greeks had committed the crime, but Greece had most unfairly to pay a large indemnity to get rid of the Italians.

The Italians were back again in 1941, following Greece's surrender to overpowering German might. The Italians, who would most probably have annexed the islands had they won the war, tried their best to woo the Ionians. Such efforts were firmly repelled, however, to the point that postmen refused to deliver letters bearing an Italian stamp with the surcharge *Isole Ionie.* But this occupation was mild compared with what was to come. On the collapse of Italy in 1943, the Germans took over, ejecting the Italians with appalling brutality and announcing their arrival on the night of 14 September 1943 with a major air raid that did more damage to Corfu town than centuries of foreign invasions had done. With fire-bombs they destroyed the Opera House, the Library with its 80,000 volumes and damaged the neighbouring seventeenth century Flamburiari Mansion (now the Cavalieri Hotel), the Venetian barracks on the Old Fortress, and the Post Office. A substantial part of Corfu's old town was irreparably damaged. The town bears marks of its ordeal to this day.

The other grim legacy of the Germans concerned Corfiot Jews. Since the Angevin times there had been a Jewish population in Corfu town, amounting in the Venetian period to about 5,000 people. The Greeks looked down upon them but let them pursue their chosen trades. It was not until the German occupation betwen 1943 and 1944 that this ancient community was uprooted. Today, the Jewish population is numbered in hundreds instead of thousands.

Since the war, the only invasion has been peaceful, in the shape of foreign tourists who, though they may have brought prosperity, have also brought the inevitable disadvantages of mass tourism. They have also helped to bring about a social shift, with the younger generation ceasing to lead an agricultural existence, becoming instead lodging-house-keepers, bar-owners, waiters, maids, taxi-drivers.

But enough of old Corfu remains for those who choose to look for it. The town, for all its war-time scars, is still one of the most original and attractive urban settings in the Mediterranean world. In the inland mountain villages in the north and centre, the pace of life has changed comparatively little: old men continue to play tric-trac at tables in the *platea,* old women seated at their doorways spin wool, donkeys laden with firewood and bundles of hay move slowly along the narrow cobbled streets. And everywhere the unoffending visitor is sure of the traditional Ionian welcome and courtesy which so beguiled earlier travellers and seekers after beauty.

The name of the Italian general was Tellini.
The British representative on the boundary commission
was Colonel Frank Giles, RE, father of the present writer.

Currency issued only for the Ionian Islands during the Italian occupation of Greece during the Second World War.

The 17th century Flamburiari Mansion, now the Cavalieri Hotel. From a drawing by Ken Reilly.

Opposite page. A typical Corfiot street scene showing tall, narrow houses, their balconies overflowing with laundry hanging out to dry.

5 The Grand Old Estates

Countess Flamburiari

The island of Corfu has been particularly blessed with a fine selection of old buildings, whether they be ancient farmhouses or grand dwellings - *Arhontika* as they are known in Greek. Unlike its sister island Zakinthos (Zante) and Cephalonia, Corfu has been miraculously spared the horror and destruction of its architectural inheritance by earthquakes.

Grand Venetian and neo-classical mansions are spread around Corfu town, surrounded by a uniquely lush landscape whose beauty has remained virtually unchanged over the centuries.

This essay cannot possibly present every estate, mansion or building of interest. The variety is enormous; so is the history they have carried with them over the centuries. I will therefore confine myself to exploring at length a mere handful of the Grand Old Estates, though not before briefly listing a few of the distinguished buildings and estates that lack of space forbids me to describe. These include the Boulgari house at Gastouri; the sixteenth-century Giallina mansion at Kavalouri; the Ventoura and Palatianos residences in Corfu town; the Trivoli, Lavranos, Ralli, Scarpa, Pierri, Theotoki and Capodistria estates; the picturesque Bogdanos villa overlooking the sea at Skondrou in Pyrgi; the Corfu town mansion of the Flamburiari family (now the Cavalieri Hotel); the Laskari building; the old Reading Society; and the historic building situated near the Palace of St George and St Michael in town, where the first Prime Minister of Greece, John Capodistrias, was born.

I thus leave the reader ample scope to search out and enjoy those mentioned here as she or he roams the island. Although these houses are not open to the public, they may be visited by private arrangement with the owners.

With its weathered roof of Roman tiles and its rusty pink Venetian facade, Afra must surely be the 'Jewel in the Crown' of Corfu's grand old estates. A square garden divided by a wide path which runs up to the entrance of the house boasts fine old Magnolia trees, orange blossom and exotic plants from the east.

*Opposite page.
A covered portico with timbered ceiling, old flagstones and an iron gate lead to the front garden of the house at Afra.*

The famous "long gallery" at Afra with its colourful stained glass window surrounds, its hunting crops which line the walls and its beautiful old painted floor tiles. All the important ground floor rooms lead off this gallery.

The dining room, with its deep mulberry red walls and its English and Venetian furniture is the hub of life at Afra. Here guests gather and Mr. Piero Curcumelli-Rodostamo usually sits, surrounded by portraits of his forebears.

AFRA
THE ROMANTIC ESTATE

Possibly the most famous and romantic of all the Grand Old Estates is Afra, still inhabited by descendants of the Rodostamo and Curcumelli families. Originally from Northern Greece, Giovanni Curcumelli arrived in Corfu from Cephalonia in 1750 to escape Turkish persecution. He built his home on the ruins of a thirteenth-century monastery.

The estate, approximately 6 kilometres north-west of Corfu town, runs to two thousand acres, and the valley stretches far beyond the grounds surrounding the house. Parts of the old monastery remain; on the ground floor of the house was the site of the nunnery, while below the staircase leading to the front door, original arches and columns can still be seen.

Until the outbreak of the Second World War, Afra enjoyed a feudal system, as inhabitants of the farms dotted about the estate all owed allegiance to the lord of the manor. Olives were cultivated here on a large scale until the end of the nineteenth century.

As you come up the ancient driveway, bumping your way over uneven, moss-grown stones, the old outside walls with their iron hay-racks (once used to feed carriage horses) rise up and surround the house with their stony embrace.

Olive-trees and cypresses flank the drive and lead to a clearing. A covered portico and an old iron gate lead to a big square garden. Tall magnolia trees scent the air and strange exotic plants, brought back from long-ago voyages to China and Japan, blossom in between ancient stone heads placed at intervals along the wide path leading up to the house. This much-photographed and lauded building, with its wonderfully rich, dark Venetian pink façade and its white framed and curved windows bordered with multicoloured glass, has become an island legend.

The main house was constructed in four stages, culminating two hundred years ago. Service quarters and store-rooms are arranged over two long side wings. All buildings on the estate, including the remains of an old olive press, are classified as historic monuments.

Once inside the house, formal ground-floor rooms lead off a long tiled corridor. There are prints of horses on the walls, racks of hunting crops and a collection of walking sticks waiting, it would seem, for their long-departed owners to select one and go out for a leisurely stroll round the estate. Lanterns of Venetian glass and wrought metal lead us to the dining-room, study, palatial drawing-room and gun-room.

Left. A little corner of Afra showing a family portrait and photographs of Victorian and Edwardian relatives.

Right. The main bedroom at Afra, where an old gilt mirror reflects a fine pair of brass bedsteads still used by present members of the family.

The grand salon, or main drawing room, takes up a good deal of the ground floor space. Venetian bookcases and important pictures are dominated at one end of the room by a large portrait of Polemnia Scaramanga, painted in Moscow by the Tsar's Court portraitist. Old fashioned lamps, a leopard skin and handsome pieces of furniture complete the decor.

*Opposite page.
At the back of the house, an unusual study of the wooden shutters and wrought iron balconies of the building, with its surrounding greenery.*

The most frequently used room in the house is the dining-room, with its rusty mulberry-red walls and English and Venetian furniture. A seventeenth-century family protrait of Matheos Rodostamo hangs over the marble fireplace in an impressive gilt frame. His benign ghost is said to make an occasional appearance. Even on a normal, sunny day, his heavy-lidded eyes, beneath his full curled wig, follow one around the room in a mildly disconcerting manner. A mahogany table piled with books and an old easy chair drawn up to the fire remind frequent visitors to Afra of Mary Curcumelli, neé Flamburiari, who died in 1991, the mother of the present owner. On the peeling walls a number of family portraits combine to make this a very much lived-in corner of the house.

In the grand salon a huge portrait of Polimnia Scaramanga, a Curcumelli ancestor painted in Moscow in the early nineteenth century by the Tsar's portraitist, dominates one part of the softly lit room. The men of the family have handed down their birthright from generation to generation, as can be seen from a close inspection of the family tree, but the women have come from far and wide. Some have been English, others Russian or Italian.

In the basement the huge antiquated kitchen - no modern contraptions here - reminds us of days gone by as we pause by the wood-burning hearth and try to imagine the hurry and bustle of the servants as they basted some slow-turning carcass of meat on the spit.

Edward Lear's diaries make several mentions of Afra. For example, in the 1860s Lear writes:

On the 22nd of May I went out very early to Signor Curcumelli - my former landlord - and I only returned last night ... The run into the country has done me a good deal of good; just about Curcumelli's house the country is too cultivated to be very picturesque, but half a mile off there are very wild scenes, of olive groves - great spreading trees, with the hills of Aghios Yiorgos peeping between. Early yesterday morning I had a very nice ride; the ground was quite dazzling; covered with rose coloured cistus, & pink everlasting peas besides innumerable large white convolvuses. The Curcumellis are very agreeable and good natured, & remind me of days passed with the Buonapartes & others in Italy. *

The interior of Afra has changed little since Giovanni Curcumelli's time, and the loving care lavished upon it by the present owner and descendant of the family, Piero Curcumelli, has helped to preserve furniture, pictures and rare books relating to different periods in the island's history. May he continue his good and painstaking work for many years to come.

* *Sir Demetrius Curcumelli, KCMG, head of the family during Lear's sojourn on the island, and his first landlord in Corfu, was Regent of Corfu in 1864 and presented the parting British garrison with the Municipal Council's farewell tribute.*

View from the long verandah at San Stefano, showing the private family chapel silhouetted against the sea.

The Justiniani and Flamburiari family crests.

SAN STEFANO
AT BENITSES

Opposite page.
The charming old villa of San Stefano at Benitses, built on a rock overlooking the sea.

Situated only 12 kilometres from the town of Corfu, San Stefano was built by a cousin of the Flamburiari family, Anneti-Justiniani-Kazamayor, in 1782.

The house and farm in the hills above the little town of Benitses is owned today by Stephen Manessis, a cousin of Piero Curcumelli at Afra and a descendant of the Flamburiaris. The Manessis became its owners in the latter part of the nineteenth century.

At this time, as the family were often abroad, the house had periods of being leased as a monastery or convent, most notably to an aunt of Tsar Nicholas II who donated the beautiful Russian icon still to be seen in the private chapel. She was an Abbess who came with her nuns to Corfu. The large stables were then used as cells for monks and nuns.

Sitting squarely on a huge grey rock, the house dominates the whole area. Once the centre of a vast agricultural estate, parts of the building are connected by cat-walks, staircases and verandahs. The house itself is approached from the main road which runs by the sea up a long, narrow, winding path. Tall trees, mostly cypresses, meet above and the cautious visitor feels that this road was never intended for anything more than the horse-drawn equipages of another era.

As we draw up to the front door, the beauty of this fine old home strikes us. The first sight is of a glorious Venetian pink facade with window and door surrounds picked out in brilliant white. Opposite the front door is an old Venetian fountain in daily use. Ancient stone heads grimace from the wall of the pink fountain, and

Another view of San Stefano, showing the rich mottled pink of its walls.

The drawing room at San Stefano, showing the old beamed ceiling and multi-coloured glass doors.

garden hoses affixed to taps protrude from their mouths. A tangle of plants and herbs in gaily - coloured pots make us aware that this old home has moved smoothly into the modern age without having to change very much and is still playing a useful, down-to-earth working role in everyday life.

Stephen Manessis, his wife Jan and their two small boys spill out of the house and welcome us indoors. The two-storey building has eighteen rooms, the most notable a living-room that boasts eleven doors and windows. Much of the furniture and all the Flamburiari family portraits and family tree have been here for many decades. Upstairs in the main bedroom is an antique carved wooden bed where countless members of the family were born and others died. Along the corridor is a charming old blue

and white porcelain lavatory which never fails to be pointed out to visitors.

On the same floor is an interesting "smuggler's door". In the bad old days, when there was always a danger of the house being raided, this door would be hastily lowered and bolted, thus closing access by the stairs to the upper floor. The family would then take refuge in the attic above and throw missiles down upon the intruders' heads should they manage to break through the door.

Our host shows us around enthusiastically, pointing out every detail of the large high-ceilinged kitchen, only slightly changed since the last century and replete with a fine family of Corfiot cats, kept firmly under the caring eye of Georgia, a beloved family retainer.

Stephen Manessis, present incumbent of the villa San Stefano, is an enthusiastic farmer and bee keeper.

A turkey at San Stefano enjoys the sun.

Opposite page.
A corner of an old bedroom showing the typical Venetian wall colour and section of a bed where generations of the Flamburiari family were born and died.

The huge old family Bible with its fine illustrations is of great interest to us, as is the visitors book, started in 1896, which reads like an international Who's Who. The more recent history of this fascinating house can be traced from the many and varied visitors whose names grace the pages of this substantial book. Some of the eminent travellers include the Empress Elisabeth of Austria, according to a note from Count George Flamburiari and his wife, who entertained her here for tea, Kaiser Wilhelm II, Queen Alexandra when she was still Princess of Wales, King George I of Greece, the entire Greek royal family in April 1900, and King George II of Greece in 1926. Later years bring the names of Vivien Leigh, Gerald Durrell, Theodore Stephanides, Peggy Guggenheim, Cecil Day-Lewis, the conductor Thomas Schippers, Prince Carl and Princess Yvonne of Hesse, and countless others.

Outside on the long covered verandah much of the daily life at San Stefano goes on. This wonderful spot is high above the sea and one never tires of the view. To the right far below is the lively little village of Benitses, while to the left is a wooded area, part of the estate. In the luxuriant garden below, olive, citrus and quince-trees enjoy the sun.

Just under the rock that supports the main house is a private chapel with a typical Corfiot bell-tower. It was recently discovered, when repairs were carried out, that one of the three bells was Byzantine, one Venetian and one Corfiot. The grace of the tower's silhouette with the deep blue of the sea behind lingers as a cherished memory.

The church may pre-date the house, but nobody is certain if the church of St Stephen in Benitses, mentioned in ecclesiastic records in the sixteenth century, is this church or a previous one. Inside the chapel, where a service is still held every year on the patron Saint's day, are tombs of the Justiniani and Flamburiari families. Indeed, until early this century burials were permitted here. Also to be seen is some fine fresco work, and icons dating from the construction of the chapel in 1782.

Left. A colourful corner of the kitchen, little changed over the years.

Right. The main bathroom at the villa San Stefano.

Copper moulds, once in daily use, here become a decorative part of tradition in old Corfiot kitchens.

The study at San Stefano.

Portraits of the Flamburiari family ancestors.

THE FORTRESS AT KOULOURA

*Opposite page.
Famous view from above the main
road looking down at Kouloura*

Once upon a time, a very long while ago, this strange house was named "Caragol" and was handed down from generation to generation of the Cartano family. In 1986 it was purchased from the last descendant by an Italian, Dr. Giorgio Marsan and his charming wife Umberta. Finding the house in a considerable state of disrepair, its new owners quickly set about transforming both house and estate into a thing of beauty.

Originally an old fortress, some 25 kms N.E. of Corfu, built some time in the early sixteenth century, this house has become a fascinating and original home, with its four look-out turrets and a vaulted cellar where the rough waves pound eternally between old stone walls. Known as "the dungeon", but as far as we know, not used as such, this is the oldest part of the building with its original paved

floor. One feels that the rumours of smugglers having made use of the dungeon in olden times were probably correct.

As we approach the main house up a flight of steps, the Quaranto coat of arms in glistening white stone is strategically placed above the front door. White walls and painted white wooden ceilings fashioned in the old Corfiot manner meet our gaze as Dr. Marsan beckons us indoors. One of the old turrets has been imaginatively transformed into a bathroom, another into a cupboard leading onto the wide verandah where life, especially during the summer months, revolves from morning to night. A turret at each end, this has been handsomely laid out for relaxing, eating, or enjoying a welcome drink at the end of the day. Far in the distance a familiar silhouette can be sighted through the heat haze. It is an identical

A blissful spot on a verandah overlooking the sea.

fortress to this one, but it is in Albania and has been allowed to go to ruin.

Dr. and Mrs. Marsan have lovingly created a Corfiot-Venetian decor using mostly Greek, Italian and English antique furniture and artefacts. Every room is simple, yet includes charming details which seem just right for these old rooms. A fine silhouette picture of Lord Byron; an old iron bedstead carefully restored; maple wood picture frames and cheerful fabrics all lend a warm and happy atmosphere to what has become a lovely home.

In the garden a series of terraces planted with trees and shrubs lean gently towards the sea. Citrus trees and oleander blossom, fruit trees and brilliantly-hued bougainvillaea everywhere all weave their perfumed magic. A shimmering

blue swimming pool, a new addition to the property, is poised above the sea in such a way as to make the swimmer feel that the pool merges with it and becomes one big blue expanse for him to enjoy.

As we turn away from house, pool and gardens, ready for our return to Corfu town, we look down at the little fishing village built in the shape of a crescent which gives Kouloura its name. This tiny village on the north eastern tip of the island is well known as one of the beauty spots of Corfu.

Just outside the main gates of the house is a restored medieval chapel also belonging to the property, while on the hills above thickly wooded land protects the approach to a fine home.

Opposite page.
View of the flower-lined courtyard at Kouloura.

View down a marble floored corridor at Kouloura.

A bedroom at Kouloura, pinpointing the Marsans' attention to detail by using period furniture and old prints.

Opposite page:
Top. Another bedroom at Kouloura. This one boasts a typical old Corfiot wooden ceiling

Bottom. The dining room at Kouloura.

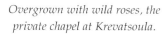

Overgrown with wild roses, the private chapel at Krevatsoula.

KREVATSOULA

Opposite page.
Through the old stone archway and into the magical world of Krevatsoula.

Originally a Venetian castle, this handsome building was bought by Nicholas Theotoki when he left Constantinople four hundred years ago and decided to settle in Corfu. The building was converted at this time into the house we see today.

Even now, nobody knows the exact date the original Venetian castle was built, but it was probably used as a fortress in its early days. This theory is borne out by the thickness of the outside walls and the presence of loop-holes in different parts of the house facing out to sea.

Set in 250 acres - one thousand stremmas - of land, the house is surrounded by approximately three thousand olive trees. Potatoes are grown and farm animals are raised here.

The house, 11 kms from Corfu, cannot be seen from the main Corfu town to Ipsos road, and it is with a feeling of uncertainty that we turn into a long drive simply marked by two stone gateposts. Green leafy trees embrace over our heads and everywhere there is a sense of being drawn back into some other time. Eventually the walled house is reached. Just by the entrance is an old monastery with a characteristic bell tower, similar to the one at St. Stefano. Wild roses and giant cactus vie with each other and merge with olive and cypress trees growing almost up to the very roof. An ancient door is set in a stone arch with an intricate brass knocker. We are welcomed through a covered passage into the yard, the house extending round three sides of it. Plants and flowers grow in profusion everywhere. The summer sun glints through a

A view of Krevatsoula from the sea.

Opposite page.
A shuttered window on the sunny
side of Krevatsoula.

This leafy courtyard heralds the entrance to the villa.

The splendid living room at Krevatsoula, with its old wooden ceiling, parquet floors, fine oriental carpets and antique furniture.

density of shrubs and dapples the old stones where we walk. A typical Venetian flight of lichen-covered stone steps leads us into this magnificent building. There are ten main rooms and auxiliary domestic quarters ranging over two floors. Our delightful hostess, Mrs. Bia Kritikou-Theotoki, invites us into the main living room. This is a vast space with high old wooden ceilings fashioned in the traditional Corfiot style always used in important dwellings of the period. Here are fine pieces of antique furniture beautifully looked after and set off to perfection in the place they were always intended for. These treasures have been collected over a period of four hundred years, and although some pieces were sadly destroyed during the Italian-German occupation of the second world war, consecutive owners have

managed to replace some pieces. At some point various objects were purchased by members of the Greek Royal family, who were frequent visitors here. King George II especially enjoyed a swim from the small beach located on the east side of the property when staying at the Villa Mimbelli nearby.

In one corner of the vast drawing room is an old Italian clay stove standing at least five feet up from the floor. Apart from being wonderfully warm in winter, this makes an unusual decoration at any time of year. Tables crowded with sepia photographs of grand figures in top hats and Victorian ball gowns, solemn portraits of past generations of the Theotoki family grace the walls and the mellow polish of brass and wood make this home both warm and

A comfortable corner in one of Krevatsoula's grand reception rooms.

A trio of silver statuettes stands out against an old willow-pattern plate.

fascinating. Although much of the drawing room furniture is Venetian, the dining room is mainly English with a fine mahogany table and chairs, while from the ceiling hangs on dull brass chains an old china Corfiot lamp.

As our hostess accompanied us out into the sunshine, I asked if she knew why the house had been named Krevatsoula, and she replied that this word alluded to the branches that the vines rested upon.

Once again down the drive and into the rush of holiday makers on the main road, my mind and senses still full of the magic cast by our visit to Krevatsoula, I wondered for how much longer Dr. and Mrs. Kritikou-Theotoki would be able to support the tremendous maintenance charges necessary to keep their lovely home from deteriorating. All the *"Arhontika"* on Corfu face the same fate, and one can only be glad of having had the opportunity of glimpsing them before the night sets in.

Fine detail from an eighteenth-
century fan at Krevatsoula.

Antique silver ornaments decorate a table in the living room at Krevatsoula.

Left. Professor Augustus Sordinas, owner of Kothoniki, in the garden with a part from one of his beloved olive presses.

Right. Imposing Venetian gateposts guard the entrance to the Kothoniki estate.

KOTHONIKI
THE WALLED ESTATE

*Opposite page.
The house at Kothoniki.*

Down a quiet country road flanked by cypresses and green leafy bushes, beyond the little village of Viros, you will come upon Kothoniki, home of the Sordinas family since the early seventeenth century.

A high wall protects the house from the road, where an imposing pair of tall Venetian gateposts is surmounted by stone vases from which sprout geraniums rising like scarlet flames towards the sky. A faded May-day garland hangs lopsidedly from wrought-iron gates. The house itself is a stone coloured Venetian villa with an outside staircase flanked all the way up by plant pots brimming over with green things and leading to the first floor. Once inside the front door, standing in the narrow hall, we are greeted by the present owner of Kothoniki, Dr. Augustus Sordinas, Professor of the Ionian University, and his American wife. They offer us a delicious fresh lemonade pressed from the glorious lemons which abound in the garden. The three main downstairs rooms are covered with books on virtually every subject. Shelves rising from floor to ceiling include the works of Freud and Hemingway as well as tomes on History, Archeology, Anthropology, travel and many other subjects which have appealed to the

Professor at some time or another. In the central room, a study, sits a large old desk with a cluster of tiny drawers, while the walls above it are lined with diplomas and faded photographs. My eyes rest upon one of the laden bookshelves and spy a long winding snakeskin which has been pinned to it. A bearer of good luck, they say. Between two of the book-bedecked rooms a tiny pair of scales such as those always linked to the figure of Justice is suspended, making us wonder what the Professor had in mind when he placed them there. The balance of good and evil, perhaps; of fair or foul play, who knows. The Professor himself, a man of so many parts, is dressed in blue denim and sports a neat white beard and colourful cotton headband. He is cheerful and lithe of foot as he leads us upstairs to a veritable treasure trove of the past.

Once the door has been opened onto a hall and long corridor one feels immediately transported into another century. There is nothing to mar this impression; every detail relates to the past. It is only within the last fifteen years that water, electricity and telephone have been installed here, yet they have not been allowed to intrude too much on the backs of centuries well used to doing without such modern innovations. In the

Luscious fruit lies at the foot of prolific trees on the estate at Kothoniki.

upstairs hallway Venetian furniture, a fine mirror and a huge Ming plate on the wall spark the visitor's interest, while in one of the rooms leading off the corridor glass cases of West African art, utensils, tools and beads, Ashanti weights and Mexican 'finds' tell us still more of our host's pursuits.

The most fascinating room of the villa, however, is the large dining room, seemingly untouched over the years. This room houses the oldest and rarest pieces of furniture. Fine Persian carpets cover the floors and, as in most of the rooms, there is a traditional old Corfiot wooden ceiling. Original Empire dining chairs with curiously curved backs steal the show and imprint their unique character on the room. On chains hanging low above the dining table is a remarkable lamp; probably designed during the transition period from candles to oil burning lamps, it boasts both clusters of candelabra on four sides and a central oil lamp. Rare blue and white china platters and dusty Venetian prints embellish the walls, while in another room a 'Portantina' - an open sedan chair - sits patiently waiting for a passenger.

Family portraits of the Counts of Corfu and Mazzarbo look down from walls surmounted by coats of arms, reminders of the days during the Turkish occupation of the mainland Greece when the inhabitants of the Ionian islands made a point of speaking Italian and using their Venetian titles.

Outside in the dappling sunshine banks of wistaria interspersed with bougainvillaea and wild roses wind unchecked and unchartered over garden and walls. The old olive press is heavy with ivy, and houses a selection of Sordinas cats. Also near the main building is a great stone tithe barn, subsiding gently into the ground, flora and fauna creeping up ever so gently to cover its traces. Wild plants for sustenance are grown here and the lemon trees with their masses of fruit are everywhere.

In the cobbled courtyard is the Sordinas family chapel, and outside the high walls surrounding the house nestles a small village. In the old days the family gave sanctuary to fugitives from the law, for which valuable service they charged a handsome fee. The family also had the monopoly in Corfu for the local salt pans.

Professor Sordinas's study, its walls packed with certificates and faded photographs, the desk piled high with papers.

Opposite page. The dining room at Kothoniki. Above the table hangs an old lamp cunningly designed to burn both oil and candles.

*A view of Mon Repos in earlier
days, painted by Anton Schranz
in the nineteenth century.
Private collection.*

Left. Mon Repos photographed from the sea.

Right. Side view of Mon Repos showing bay windows which have a view over the rose garden.

Below. Detail of an ornate lantern outside Mon Repos.

MON REPOS
THE SUMMER PALACE

The story of Mon Repos began in 1828, when Lady (Nina) Palatianos-Adam asked her husband, Sir Frederick, the second High Commissioner, to build a summer palace for the High Commissioners of the Ionian Islands. The offcial name given at that time to the palace was "the House of St Pandeleimon", as it had been built on the ruins of a church bearing this name. However, the name finally chosen by the Lord High Commissioner and Lady Adam, his Corfiot-born wife, was "The Casino".

The building, in the neo-classical Regency style, was started in 1828 and was ready for occupation by 1831. The architect was Sir George Whitmore, also responsible for the Palace of St Michael and St George in Corfu.

Situated just outside Corfu town between Garitsa and Analipsis, and built near the ancient city of Paleopolis, now an archaeological site, the palace gates with their deep ochre arches and palm-trees can easily be seen from the main road.

Sadly for Sir Frederick Adam and his wife, "The Casino" was never enjoyed by them, as before its completion they left for India, where he was to become Governor of Madras. After Adam's departure, his successor Lord Nugent suggested that the building should be used for some public purpose, and for a very brief period it served as a seminary. For the remaining years of the British Protectorate it was used by the Lord High Commissioner himself and by members of his staff. After the cession of Corfu to Greece in 1864 the British decided to give the palace to King George I of Greece. He in turn bequeathed it to Prince Andrew of Greece, who eventually sold it to King George II of Greece. By this time the building had been re-named "Mon Repos". It was here, in 1921, that Prince Philip, Duke of Edinburgh, was born.

An old print of Mon Repos in its days of glory as the British High Commissioner's villa.

Opposite page.
A closer look at Mon Repos as it stands today.

After the plebiscite in 1974 which established a Republic, the beautifully proportioned Regency building fell into disrepair. Many pieces of furniture were plundered, others sold or sent away to other houses. The beautiful columns and generous bay-fronted windows are quite abandoned now.

Lovely even in decay, the romantic gardens with their profusion of rose bushes spill down to the sea.

Across the bay is Corfu town, yet around the palace the wild foliage creeps higher with each passing year. A beautiful little chapel hides in a remote corner of the grounds, all blue and white inside, where Kings and Queens and Princes once worshipped. Now the cobwebs shroud the altar,

and a sleepy bat is startled into motion by the stranger's step.

At Mon Repos one year, King George I of Greece and the then Prince of Wales, later Edward VII, fought a duel in the garden with over-ripe oranges. King George once jested wryly that he planned to be in residence in Corfu whenever the Kaiser stayed there - "Because if I don't, he will think he's the King of Greece!"

Lord Louis Mountbatten was a frequent guest, and the young Crown Prince Alexander of Yugoslavia passed many a carefree summer here with his Greek cousins. Prince Juan Carlos of Spain came before his engagement to Princess Sofia of Greece. What better spot to sow the seeds of a romantic future?

6 The Empress Elisabeth and the Achilleion

Major J. K. Forte MBE

In May 1861 a beautiful, fairylike young Queen fell in love at first sight with the magical island of Corfu, where she dreamed of building a fairy palace in which to live happily ever after. Her name was Elisabeth and she was the daughter of Duke Max of Bavaria and Ludovica Wittelsbach, his second cousin.

The Wittelsbachs deserve a whole page to themselves in the *Guinness Book of Records*, for not only had they ruled over Bavaria for more than seven centuries, but generation after generation had married into the royal cousinhood, thereby infusing a streak of Wittelsbach blood into practically every crowned head in Europe, including Greece, where in the first part of the nineteenth century King Otto ruled over what he described as his "bandit subjects". Furthermore some thirty-five generations of interbreeding among cousins had resulted in the Wittelsbachs establishing a race of their own apart, sometimes

hallmarked by genius but at all times by eccentricity, and occasionally insanity. However, Duke Max's marriage was the first time that Wittelsbach had actually married Wittelsbach, bequeathing to Elisabeth dangerously unstable gifts whose traits were only enhanced by her own marriage in 1854 at the age of sixteen to her first cousin, the twenty-four-year-old Emperor Franz Joseph of Austria.

It was perhaps hardly surprising that the match between the two Wittelsbachs should give issue to a highly-strung, nervous, excitable, unbalanced hypochondriac whose fits of melancholia and depression in a well of loneliness were tempered with spasms of delightful gaiety and immense *joie de vivre,* with a facility for combining royal dignity with girlish simplicity. What was less predictable was that the union should also produce one of the legendary beauties of all time.

The Achilleion, a fairy palace built as an escape from life at the Austrian court by the Empress Elisabeth of Austria.

unfaithful, but had also contaminated her.

On arrival in Corfu, the Empress felt sorely tempted to accept the offer of the Lord High Commissioner, Colonel Sir Henry Storks, to avail herself of his summer villa Mon Repos on the outskirts of the town; but her schedule would not allow her to dally longer than twenty-four hours, since she was committed to being reunited with her repentant husband, still very much in love with her, and already on his way from Vienna to meet her at sea off Trieste. Nevertheless her stay was long enough to enable her to sample the legendary properties of the waters of the Kardaki spring hard by Mon Repos, which compel the drinker willy-nilly to return to the island.

If Sir Henry felt gratified not to have been turfed out of his summer residence he must have failed to show his gratitude to Saint Spyridon, for within six weeks the Empress was back again, this time to take up his offer and to sow the seeds for the realisation of her dream. Life in Vienna had become unbearable and her health had seriously deteriorated. Dr Skoda, her personal physician, predicted that if she stayed on in the city she would be dead in six weeks. Various remedial spas were suggested, but Elisabeth's mind had long since been made up.

In his dispatch dated 30 June, Lord Blomfield, the British Ambassador, reported: "I fear she has gone to Corfu to die". However, Corfiot therapy, which included the improbable pursuit of swimming and sailing far out to sea, sitting outdoors at night-time to admire the moonlight, listening to the chattering of the crickets and the tuneful hoot of the night owl, worked miracles; and by the end of July Dr Skoda was able to report a marked improvement in the health of the Empress.

No mention was made of any intention of her leaving for Vienna, but after months of pleading by her family Elisabeth consented to return home on 13 October and a concerned Emperor arrived to escort her back. On her next visit she would find Corfu under new management, for nineteen months later the Ionian Islands were ceded to Greece.

Seven years of matrimony had resulted for Elisabeth in disillusionment with her marriage and an urge to flee from her duties and obligations in Vienna. So here she was on that fateful morning in May 1861, disembarking at Corfu from the yacht *Victoria and Albert* to discover a new goal in life that would help to mend her heart, broken by the unnecessary death of her three-year-old eldest daughter, Sofia. The most luxurious of all the English royal yachts had been loaned to her by Queen Victoria to convey her home by easy stages from Madeira, where she had wintered in the hope that its warm sunshine would have a beneficial effect on her ill health. This was officially diagnosed as anaemic consumption, but Elisabeth realised that she was in fact suffering from an unpleasant contagious disease passed on by a husband who had not only been

We next hear of Elisabeth stopping off in Corfu on a whirlwind tour of Greece in 1877, when she found the island more enchanting and captivating than ever. However it was not until ten years later that she instructed Baron Warsburg, the Austrian Consul, to keep an eye out for a suitable property to buy. The one he selected was a charming pink-painted villa with patios covered by vines and bougainvillaea surrounded by an expanse of olives, oranges, lemons and wild flowers. It was situated 9 kilometres south of the town on the outskirts of the village of Gastouri, just above the coastal road to the nearby fishing village of Benitses. A succession of cypress-clad terraces led down to the sea, with the Albanian mountains in the background.

The property was owned by a Corfiot philosopher, politician and diplomat named Petros Vrailas Armenis and went by the name of "Villa Vraila". As soon as Elisabeth inspected the place in the autumn of 1888 she decided it was the perfect site for her dream fairy palace. Warsburg had already been appointed her guide and mentor on her tour round the Ionian Islands on previous occasions, and had so enthralled her with tales of Homer that she had become completely infatuated with Achilles in the process. As she later confided to her Greek tutor Christomanos, "I dedicated the Achilleion to him because for me he represents the very soul of Greece, the fairness of its land and glamour of its manhood. Yet I love him because he was as wing-footed as Hermes, powerful, proud and

The Achilleion viewed from the sea, with the village of Benitses nestling below.

View from the gardens and terrace of the Achilleion over the sea.

*Opposite page.
Classical gods and goddesses line one wall of the palace facing the garden.*

obstinate like a Greek mountain, and disdaining all laws, despising all mortals, he did not even fear the gods".

When she commissioned Warsburg to build her a Phaeacian palace dedicated to her hero, Elisabeth instructed : "I want a palace with pillared colonnades and hanging gardens, safe from prying eyes - a palace worthy of Achilles". No commission could have been more beguiling to a man who had spent a lifetime in studying the legends of the Ionian Islands. In building the Achilleion - whose classical features are copied from models of the city of Pompeii, destroyed by the eruption of Vesuvius in AD79 - Warsburg, who was assisted by the Neapolitan architect Rafael Carito, gratified Elisabeth's every whim, from the marble baths with gilded taps supplying warmed pumped sea-water, to the naked Eros climbing the toilet cistern, whilst everywhere would be found the stamp of Greek mythology. No expense was spared. Academicians from Vienna, sculptors and stucco workers from Italy were summoned to Corfu to create an atmosphere of Greek antiquity. As a final grace note, every item of

porcelain (including the chamber-pots), silver and glass, even the bed-linen and note paper, had to bear the crest of a dolphin surmounted by the Imperial crown, the dolphin being sacred to the sea-nymph Thetis, the mother of Achilles.

But what most impressed the local inhabitants was the illumination of the whole (in particular the statues) by the island's first-ever generated electricity, which was hailed as pure magic. Sadly Baron Warsburg did not live to see the day when the Achilleion would be anywhere near completed, and this task was left to the Austrian naval architect Baron von Bucovich, who enlisted the help of another Neapolitan, Antonio Landi. If the finished product has been branded by intellectual pundits as a Germanic monstrosity in the worst of taste it nevertheless found royal favour not only with the Empress Elisabeth of Austria but also with King George I of the Hellenes and the Emperor Wilhelm II of Germany, while contemporary tourists viewing the palace from the sea, gleaming white amongst the cypresses and myrtles, regarded it as "marvellous and unique".

This coat of arms remains as a reminder of Imperial splendour of times gone by.

In the spring of 1891, inspired by Warsburg, Elisabeth began to study both modern and ancient Greek with a Corfiot tutor recommended by him named Constantinos Christomanos, who was studying at Vienna University. He was a delicate, deformed, hunchback who appealed to Elisabeth at first sight. There seems to have been a streak of perversity in her character which attracted freaks. During the previous decade she had been presented by the Khedive of Egypt with a spectacularly ugly black servant named Rustimo, whom she dressed up in royal livery and bade to wait at table. It provided great sport for her to watch fastidious guests wince and shudder in disgust when he removed the dinner plates with his clumsy fingers, sometimes spilling the leftovers upon them. On one occasion in a bored mood she offered her lady-in-waiting, Marie Walersee, a valuable brooch if she could bring herself to kiss Rustimo, whereupon she grabbed him smartly and planted a kiss on each cheek. This made the little grotesque so cocky that he literally created panic amongst the chambermaids, chasing them up and down the corridors and in and out of the bedrooms.

Christomanos was at Elisabeth's beck and call every hour of the day, reading aloud to her from the classics. Installed in the Hofburg in Vienna, at meals he would recount the Homeric legends. The literary menu was the same at breakfast and luncheon, and though Elisabeth's appetite could never be satisfied, the Emperor soon became bored stiff with the same diet at every meal.

Although Christomanos accompanied Elisabeth abroad on all her travels to escape from reality it was not until the spring of 1892 that he travelled to Corfu with her; for the Achilleion had only just, at long last, been completed. Together they explored the countryside, dispensing with bodyguards and ladies-in-waiting. They became a familiar sight amongst the peasants - the tall, fast-moving, veiled Queen with her crippled companion, Homer in hand, struggling to keep up with her. They named her the "locomotive" for the speed at which she moved, and soon grew fond of the strange foreigner who would often stop for a chat and a glass of milk, which was rewarded with a piece of gold.

However, by April 1894 Elisabeth had grown bored with Christomanos, who after his dismissal went on to publish his popular journals (translated into French and German), in which he unfolds his adulation of the Empress, and the confidences she shared with him. Soon she became bored with the Achilleion too, and tried in vain to palm it off on to her favourite daughter Valerie, married with two children to her cousin the Archduke Franz Salvator. In 1896 Elisabeth visited her "fairy palace" for what proved to be the last time in a restless life plagued by tragedy, grief and loneliness. It was then that she added yet another statue to the Achilleion.

This time it was a memorial to her only son, the Crown Prince Rudolf, seven years after his supposed suicide pact with his lover Mary Vetsera, at Mayerling on 29 January 1889. Onlookers at the unveiling ceremony say that Elisabeth looked paler and more rigid than any statue.

In 1897 the Greek-Turkish war broke out, and then the following year, on 19 September 1898, the shocking news was flashed throughout the world that the Empress Elisabeth of Austria had been assassinated at the quayside of Lake Geneva by an Italian anarchist named Luigi Luceni, who thrust a makeshift dagger into her chest.

After Elisabeth's tragic death the Emperor Franz Joseph brought back Rudolf's memorial to Vienna and put the Achilleion up for sale; but only two parties expressed any interest. One was a banker who was keen to convert it into a hotel, the other a company wanting to turn the palace into a casino. However, the Emperor considered such transformation sacrilege to the memory of the Elisabeth he so much loved.

From 1898 to 1907 the Achilleion remained empty and shut. The furnishings and internal decoration deteriorated and the structure throughout suffered severely through disrepair and lack of maintenance, while the garden became a complete wilderness. However in 1905 Kaiser Wilhelm II, Emperor of Germany, another romantic with the inevitable Wittelsbach blood running through his veins (his paternal grandmother was Elisabeth's aunt Elise) appeared on the scene. In fact Wilhelm's first visit to Corfu had been in 1889, a few months after he was proclaimed Emperor and while the Achilleion was still under construction. Now he was back again staying at the palace of St Michael and St George, as the guest of King George I of the Hellenes, whose grandson Paul was to marry Wilhelm's granddaughter Frederika, the penultimate crowned Queen of Greece.

The Kaiser, in his Memoirs, describes his visit to the Achilleion: "We carried out a careful inspection of the building and wandered around the gardens, which had been badly neglected. Everywhere there was the sign and atmosphere of utter abandonment. Nevertheless I was completely stunned by the sheer beauty of the classical antiquity which surrounded me and the entrancing panorama both out to sea with the coast of Epirus in the background, and inland the beckoning enchanting countryside. Back in Corfu town the King suggested that I purchase the Achilleion as a retreat where the Empress and I could relax after the rigours of the harsh Berlin winter. He added that he personally, together with his country and government, would be more than happy to extend their hospitality in the traditional Greek manner".

This idea appealed to the Kaiser, and he wrote off straight away to Franz Joseph, who was only too pleased to accommodate. Negotiations were protracted, however, and lasted two years before agreement could be obtained with Elisabeth's daughter Gisela, Princess of Bavaria, who under her mother's will had the right to use the Achilleion during her lifetime. Thus it was not until the spring of 1908 that the Achilleion, after drastic alterations, renovation and restoration, was fit to receive its new proprietor. The Kaiser stayed there four more times, in 1909, 1910, 1912 and 1914. On each occasion he would arrive with his whole Berlin court in the middle of March and remain until the end of April.

A large, extremely solid ornamental concrete jetty, still intact today, was built as a landing stage for the imperial yacht *Hohenzollern*, from which six red Mercedes, the first-ever motorcars to appear on the island, would be offloaded to carry the royal party in convoy up to the Achilleion, 4 kilometres away. A shorter cut for those carrying the household bundles was via a specially constructed foot-bridge over the road which connected the jetty directly with the property. Although subsequently demolished in 1944 to allow the passage of a huge German coastal gun beneath, the locality still bears the name "Kaiser's Bridge".

On his first holiday at the Achilleion the Greek state bestowed upon the Kaiser the honorary rank of Admiral in the Hellenic Navy, and thereafter he would strut around Corfu in a white summer uniform regardless of the fact that at that time of the year the Greek armed forces were still in winter dress. The Kaiser's favourite excursion was to the quaint village of Pelekas, 20 kilometres distant, set in the hills on the west coast and famous for its commanding view of over one-third of the island. It was almost a daily routine to drive through the village to a small pinnacle that subsequently became known as the "Kaiser's Throne" to admire the panorama and witness the spectacular sunset over the sea.

Like his cousin Elisabeth, the Kaiser was popular with the local peasantry, a large number of whom he employed on the estate. Furthermore, the royal band would play alongside the band of the nearby villages while his daughter (later to become the mother of Greece's Queen Frederika) joined in the Greek dancing. He would also participate in the local Easter festivities. But perhaps he is best remembered in Corfu for taking a personal interest in its excavations and for summoning the eminent German archaeoligist Dörpfeld to unearth the island's most important finds.

The story of the Achilleion is of course incomplete without a tour of the actual premises. However, this is a time-consuming exercise beyond our reach, as a description of the palace, its gardens and its works of art would occupy a whole book. Let us therefore compromise by taking a quick look around the Achilleion and a brief glance at some of the most important and interesting exhibits.

Once through the imposing wrought iron gate bearing the name Achilleion, we hasten up the drive and are able to distinguish lurking amongst the flower beds and bushes various deities such as Hermes, messenger of the gods, the poetess Sappho, Apollo, god of light, music and prophecy, Artemis, goddess of hunting and Aphrodite, goddess of love.

Our first pause is at the massive iron front door, supported by huge Doric pillars, where we are

Right. Balustrade in the main hall of the Achilleion, embellished with figures from Greek mythology.

Below. Painted walls continue the classical theme of the palace decorations.

Opposite page. A magnificent view of the grand staircase.

Detail of a richly ornamented ceiling.

Opposite page.
The famous painting of Achilles Triumphant, painted by Franz Matz and measuring eleven metres by four. It occupies the entire wall of the upper hall.

confronted by two bronze bas-reliefs, one depicting Achilles riding into battle in his four-horsed chariot and the other portraying Zeus, the supreme god, on Olympus strafing his father Kronus and fellow Titans with the thunderbolt given to him by the Cyclops.

In the spacious entrance hall is a remarkable fresco which occupies the whole centre of the vault. The work of the Italian painter Galopi, it depicts the four seasons.

At the foot of the majestic staircase Zeus himself, taking time off from thundering at the Titans, together with Hera, his spouse, stand ceremoniously in brass to welcome us into their universe.

On the ground floor are several reception rooms, three of which contain memorabilia of the Emperor and Empress. Elisabeth's Catholic chapel is open, and we peep in to admire the beautiful fresco in the centre of the ceiling painted by an unknown artist and depicting Christ before Pilate.

Also we cannot resist the temptation of entering the room containing Elisabeth's bedroom furniture. In a fine painting over the fireplace, the Bavarian artist L. Miers brings to life the daughter of King Alkinoos of the Phaeacians handing over her red tunic to the naked shipwrecked Odysseus, an event which, legend has it, took place around 1200BC at Ermones on Corfu's west coast, exactly as described in Homer.

On the second and top floor we behold the Achilleion's renowned and famous painting "Achilles Triumphant". Painted by Franz Matz, of enormous proportions measuring 11 metres by 4, it occupies the whole wall of the upper hall. The vivid scene taken from Homer's Iliad is portrayed with uncanny realism. It depicts Achilles (having killed Hector, leader of the Trojan army in a duel) standing in his chariot displaying Hector's helmet aloft in his right hand while holding his shield and spear in the other. With a great effort the charioteer endeavours to restrain the bolting black stallion galloping furiously round the walls of Troy, dragging, in a cloud of dust, Hector's dead body tied to the back of the chariot, while the entrenched Trojan soldiers look on in horror.

Descending to the upper and lower gardens, we get our first real taste of the Grecian antiquity which so entranced Kaiser Wilhelm. Here Apollo the god of music, appropriately with a lyre in his hand, introduces us to his protegés, the three graces and the nine muses. It seems surprising that Elisabeth should have had any truck with Apollo, since he it was who double-crossed her hero by revealing to Paris the secret of Achilles's vulnerable heel; whereupon Hector's brother took revenge by loosing off the fatal arrow which pierced his tendon.

It is this incident which forms the theme of the Achilleion's most important statue, the "Dying Achilles" which lies on a lower level at the end of the colonnade. It is the work of the German Ernst Herther and is a replica of a plaster sculpture which Elisabeth spotted at an exhibition in Vienna in 1881 and then commissioned in marble. Standing on an oblong base, it depicts her hero, naked but for a draped

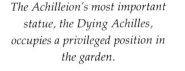

The Achilleion's most important statue, the Dying Achilles, occupies a privileged position in the garden.

loin-cloth, in a half-reclining pose with his Myrmidon's helmet on. His head is turned to his right, his right leg is bent inwards, his left leg is outstretched. His right hand is reaching out to extract the poisoned arrow and his noble face is contorted with excruciating pain which is accentuated by the tautness of his muscles expressing extreme stress.

Among the additions the Kaiser made to the Achilleion and its grounds, probably the best-known is the giant statue known as *Achilles Triumphant,* which stands in the lower gardens. It is the work of the German sculptor Godz, executed in strict accord with the Kaiser's specifications, a proud and arrogant Achilles arrayed in all his military glory. The spear and helmet are gold-plated to enable the warrior to shine from afar. The statue bore the inscription in large bronze letters:

ΑΧΙΛΛΕΥΣ
"Τόνδε 'Αχιλλῆα Πηλείδην στῆσε
Γερμανῶν κρατέων Γουλιέλμος
μνῆμα 'Επιγιγνομένοις"
This being accurately interpreted reads:

ACHILLES

This Achilles, son of Peleus, was erected by Germany's Wilhelm as a memorial for the generations to come.

The inscription was removed by the French military in 1917, but photographs of it, clearly legible at the base of the statue, bear witness to its authenticity. Despite this fact, irresponsible historians, guides and guidebooks whose ancient Greek is either rusty or more probably non-existent, have invented the rendering: "To the greatest of the Greeks from the greatest of the Germans"- a myth which naive readers and gullible tourists invariably swallow.

The giant statue known as Achilles Triumphant was an addition made by the Kaiser.

ΑΧΙΛΛΕΥΣ

Just as we are leaving the lower garden we spot, half hidden in the bushes, the stunning figure of Phryne. The legend goes that Phryne, whose admirers included artists, orators and philosophers such as Praxiteles, Hyperides and Xenocrates, was sentenced to death for continual soliciting. On pronouncement of the sentence she tore open her blouse to display her captivating form to the judges who were so "affronted" that they reversed their decision and became her "financial advisers".

In the peristyle courtyard stands the most curious and intricate statue of all, in the middle of a small pond of water-lilies. It depicts Arion, the famed musician, with a dolphin curled round his body as it rescues him from the sea. The fable is told that Arion, after winning the first European song contest held in Sicily in 625 BC, returned to Corinth with his prizes, which the captain and crew of his ship planned to steal after killing him at the end of a charity concert they had persuaded him to give. Arion managed to escape in time by leaping into the sea, whereupon he was rescued by a dolphin which had been a member of his audience. On a pedestal on the edge of the pond Dionysus is mounted on the back of a satyr, but both are so engrossed in their antics that they are completely oblivious of the drama being enacted before them.

We also spot the beautiful Leda fondly clasping a swan to her naked breast. This illustrates the myth that tells how Leda was seduced by the lecherous Zeus, who visited her in the form of a swan on the banks of the River Eurotas. Leda subsequently laid an egg, and when it hatched, out popped the fabulously beautiful Helen. We also seem to have overlooked the thirteen busts of famous philosophers, orators and poets waiting to be introduced under the colonnade. Sensibly they all have their name-tags attached, like delegates at a seminar, so there is no need to announce them, though the last in line requires no introduction as it is none other than William Shakespeare of Stratford-upon-Avon. Incidentally, the Bard is not the only intruder of the Christian era to be granted poetic licence to gate crash the domain of the heroes; Elisabeth's beloved poet Heinrich Heine, whose style of lyric she copied in her own verse, was very much in evidence during her occupancy of the Achilleion, while she also had a soft spot for Lord Byron, who is seated, wearing his familiar cape, in the lower garden.

Finally, on the edge of the estate near the sea we come across the small marble temple that originally housed the statue of Elisabeth's beloved Heine. To Kaiser Wilhelm, the poet was nothing but a subversive Jew who had dared to satirise him in public, and one of the Emperor's first acts was to get rid of the image he found so objectionable. On the empty pedestal in its stead, he placed the statue of the woman who created the Achilleion; and there she stands today, looking over the bay at the mountains of Epirus, sad, pensive and remote, still searching for the unattainable.

On 29 April 1914 the Kaiser left Corfu never to return. Maybe he had a premonition, for in his diary he writes: "We are leaving behind us a whole world which was truly wonderful . . . we hug the coast as close as we can to bid a final farewell to the Achilleion." Some three months later, on 3 August, he declared war on France, and the following day Great Britain declared war on Germany. On 9 November 1918, two days before the Armistice, the Emperor of Germany was to abdicate and escape to Doorn in Holland, where he lived in exile until his death in 1941 at the age of eighty-two.

For the next half-century the Achilleion was a dead loss in more senses than one. From the end of 1914 until 1918, when Corfu was used as an allied naval and military base, the building was requisitioned for a French military hospital. After the war it was confiscated by the Greek state as enemy property, but no effort was made to put it to any purposeful use and it became a white elephant, though the gardens were opened to the public. The more valuable furniture and art treasures were sold by auction or else mysteriously disappeared. Looting of the Kaiser's property, which was considered "fair game", continued until 1946. Today many an *objet d'art* is apt to turn up in antique shops or in the salons of the wealthy, and should it be admired the owner may be heard to announce smugly: "Ah! that came from the Achilleion".

During the Second World War the Achilleion again became a hospital, first for the Greek army, then for the Italian and finally for the German forces. After the liberation the building was put to various uses as an encampment for displaced children, a seminar centre for state teachers and a national Institute of Technology - but all the time it was gradually falling apart. Then in 1961 the Greek

government accepted a proposal by the German Baron von Richthofen (a nephew of the legendary First World War flying ace), representing foreign and Greek interests, for the conversion of the Achilleion into a casino and accordingly a twenty-year agreement was signed. The last thing the Empress of Austria and the Emperor of Germany could ever have contemplated was that one day their royal palace would be turned into a casino. It must have made them turn in their graves to watch the imperial apartments, especially the fantastic ornamental marble bathrooms with their brass dolphin headed taps gushing warm therapeutical sea-water, being demolished to make way for the gaming rooms.

Miraculously in little over a year the mammoth task was completed, and the inauguration took place at Christmas 1962 amidst much splendour, pomp and ceremony, at the end of which play commenced.

Spectacular though this lavish opening celebration may have been, it did not match the grandeur of the reception given six years later in honour of multi-billionaire L. Ron Hubbard,

founder of the Church of Scientology. This event is referred to in the official documentary entitled "The Commodore and The Colonels" which records the most sensational drama in the post-war history of Corfu. By freely disbursing his cash around Corfu, Hubbard generated a favourable climate in which to promulgate plans for the establishment of his "Church of Scientology" under the guise of a public benefactor offering to carry out a mammoth economic reconstruction and development programme for the island which would include a University of (Hubbard's) Philosophy. It was thanks largely to the international press, strongly opposed to Hubbard's activities in Corfu and reporting certain incidents perpetrated against British and U.S. nationals, which eventually jolted the authorities into ordering the sudden and immediate departure of Hubbard and his fleet from the island.

In 1983, on termination of the twenty-year lease, the casino came under control of the Greek National Tourist Organisation, and the Achilleion remains now, as then, Corfu's foremost tourist attraction.

All that remains today of the Kaiser's Bridge.

*A proud and arrogant
Achilles, arrayed in all
his military glory.*

Gerald Durrell among the ruins of an old olive press.

7 Childhood Memories

Gerald Durrell

In the 1930s, the Durrell family (Mrs Durrell, Lawrence, Leslie, Margo and Gerald) lived in Corfu in a variety of rented houses. Later, Gerald wrote three books of reminiscences about these years, the best-known of which is My Family and Other Animals. *What follows is a selection, approved by the author himself, of excerpts from those books.*

The island's shape

Corfu lies off the Albanian and Greek coast-lines like a long, rust-eroded scimitar. The hilt of the scimitar is the mountain region of the island, for the most part barren and stony with towering rock cliffs haunted by the blue rock-thrushes and peregrine falcons. In the valleys in this mountain region, however, where water gushes plentifully from the red and gold rocks, you would get forests of almond and walnut trees, casting shade as cool as a well, thick battalions of spear-like cypress and silver-trunked fig trees with leaves as large as a salver. The blade of the scimitar is made up of rolling greeny-silver eiderdowns of giant olives, some reputedly over five hundred years old, and each one unique in its hunched, arthritic shape, its trunk pitted with a hundred holes like pumice stone. Towards the tips of the blade you had Lefkimi with its twinkling, eye-aching sand dunes and great salt marshes, decorated with acres of bamboos that creaked and rustled and whispered to each other surreptitiously.

(Birds, Beasts and Relatives, *Harper Collins*, 1969)

The peaceful Corfiot countryside showing stately cypress trees against a vivid blue sea.

Scenic effects

In spring the almost enclosed sheet of water that separated Corfu from the mainland would be a pale and delicate blue; then, as spring settled into hot, crackling summer, it seemed to stain the still sea a deeper and more unreal colour that in some lights was like the violet blue of a rainbow, a blue that faded to a rich jade green in the shallows. In the evening when the sun sank it was as if it were drawing a brush across the sea's surface, streaking and blurring it to purples smudged with gold, silver, tangerine and pale pink. To look at this placid, land-locked sea in summer it seemed mild-mannered, a blue meadow that breathed gently and evenly along the shoreline; it was difficult to believe that it could be fierce; but even on a still, summer's day, somewhere in the eroded hills of the mainland, a hot fierce wind would suddenly be born and leap, screaming, at the island, turning the sea so dark it was almost black, combing each wave crest into a sheaf of white froth and urging and harrying them like a herd of panic-stricken blue horses until they crashed exhausted on the shore and died in a hissing shroud of foam. And in winter, under an iron-grey sky, the sea would lift sullen muscles of almost colourless waves, ice-cold and unfriendly, veined here and there with mud and debris that the winter rains swept out of the valleys and into the bay.

(The Garden of the Gods, *Harper Collins*, 1978)

These summer storms would be hatched in a nest of cumulus clouds in the Albanian mountains and ferried rapidly across to Corfu by a warm, scouring wind like the blast from a baker's oven ...the olives changed from green to silver like the sudden gleam of a turning school of fish, and the wind roared its way through a million leaves with a noise like a giant breaker on the shore. The blue sky was suddenly, miraculously, blotted out by bruise-coloured clouds that were splintered by jagged spears of lavender-coloured lightning. The hot, fierce wind increased and the olive groves shook and hissed as though shaken by some huge, invisible predator. Then came the rain, plummeting out of the sky in great gouts . . . a background to all this was the thunder, stalking imperiously across the sky, rumbling and snarling above the scudding clouds like a million stars colliding, crumbling and avalanching through space.

(The Garden of the Gods)

Winter came to the island gently as a rule. The sky was still clear, the sea blue and calm, and the sun warm. But there would be an uncertainty in the air. The gold and scarlet leaves that littered the countryside in great drifts whispered and chuckled among themselves, or took experimental runs from place to place, rolling like coloured hoops among the trees. It was as if they were practising something, preparing for something, and they would discuss it excitedly in rustly voices as they crowded round the tree trunks. The birds, too, congregated in little groups, puffing out their feathers, twittering thoughtfully. The whole air was one of expectation, like a vast audience waiting for the curtain to go up. Then one morning you threw back the shutters and looked down over the olive-trees, across the blue bay to the russet mountains of the mainland, and became aware that winter had arrived, for each mountain peak would be wearing a tattered skull-cap of snow. Now the air of expectancy grew almost hourly.

In a few days small white clouds started their winter parade, trooping across the sky, soft and chubby, long, languorous, and unkempt, or small and crisp as feathers, and driving them before it, like an ill-assorted flock of sheep, would come the wind. This was warm at first, and came in gentle gusts, running through the olive-groves so that the leaves trembled and turned silver with excitement, rocking the cypresses so that they undulated gently, and stirring the dead leaves into gay, swirling little dances that died as suddenly as they began. Playfully it ruffled the feathers on the sparrows' backs, so that they shuddered and fluffed themselves; and it leapt without warning at the gulls, so that they were stopped in mid-air and had to curve their white wings against it. Shutters started to bang and doors chattered suddenly in their frames. But still the sun shone, the sea remained placid, and the mountains sat complacently, summer-bronzed, wearing their splintered snow hats.

For a week or so the wind played with the island, patting it, humming to itself among the bare branches. Then there was a lull, a few days' strange calm; suddenly, when you least expected it, the wind would be back. But it was a changed wind, a mad, hooting, bellowing wind that leapt down on the island and tried to blow it into the sea. The blue sky vanished as a cloak of fine grey cloud was thrown over the island. The sea turned a deep blue, almost black, and became crusted

The blue sky was suddenly miraculously blotted out by bruise-coloured clouds.

Opposite page.
Two plump peasant girls, their chatter and laughter echoing among the olive groves.

with foam. The cypress trees were whipped like dark pendulums against the sky, and the olives (so fossilised all summer, so still and witch-like) were infected with the madness of the wind and swayed creaking on their misshapen, sinewy trunks, their leaves hissing as they turned, like mother of pearl, from green to silver. This is what the dead leaves had whispered about, this is what they had practised for; exultantly they rose in the air and danced, whirligigging about, dipping, swooping, falling exhausted when the wind tired of them and passed on. Rain followed the wind, but it was a warm rain that you could walk in and enjoy, great fat drops that rattled on the shutters, tapped on the vine leaves like drums, and gurgled musically in the gutters. The rivers up the Albanian mountains became swollen and showed white teeth in a snarl as they rushed down to the sea, tearing at their banks, grabbing the summer debris of sticks, logs, grass tussocks, and other things and disgorging them into the bay, so that the dark-blue waters became patterned with great coiling veins of mud and other flotsam. Gradually all these veins burst, and the sea changed from blue to yellow-brown; then the wind tore at the surface, piling the water into ponderous waves, like great tawny lions with white manes that stalked and leaped upon the shore.

(My Family and Other Animals
Rupert Hart-Davis, 1956)

Getting to know people

I came to know the plump peasant girls who passed the garden every morning and evening. Riding side-saddle on their slouching, drooping-eared donkeys, they were shrill and colourful as parrots, and their chatter and laughter echoed among the olive-trees. In the mornings they would smile and shout greetings as their donkeys pattered past, and in the evenings they would lean over the fuschia hedge, balancing precariously on their steeds' backs, and, smiling, hold out gifts for me - a bunch of amber grapes still sun-warmed, some figs black as tar striped with pink where they had burst their seams with ripeness, or a giant water-melon with an inside like pink ice. As the days passed, I came gradually to understand them. What had at first been a confused babble became a series of recognisable separate sounds. Then, suddenly, these took on meaning, and slowly and haltingly

A well known landmark, the tower of the church dedicated to St. Spyridon.

I started to use them myself; then I took my newly acquired words and strung them into ungrammatical and stumbling sentences. Our neighbours were delighted, as though I had conferred some delicate compliment by trying to learn their language. They would lean over the hedge, their faces screwed up with concentration, as I groped my way through a greeting or a simple remark, and when I had successfully concluded they would beam at me, nodding and smiling, and clap their hands. By degrees I learnt their names, who was related to whom, which were married and which hoped to be, and other details. I learnt where their cottages were among the olive-groves, and should Roger [Gerald's dog] and I chance to pass that way the entire family, vociferous and pleased, would tumble out to greet us, to bring a chair, so that I might sit under their vine and eat some fruit with them.

(My Family and Other Animals)

Visiting Saint Spyridon

Saint Spyridon was the patron saint of the island. His body was enshrined in a silver coffin in the church, and once a year he was carried in procession round the town.*He was very

*In fact, the ceremony takes place four times annually (Ed.).

powerful, and could grant requests, cure illness, and do a number of other wonderful things for you if he happened to be in the right mood when asked. The islanders worshipped him, and every second male on the island was called Spiro in his honour. Today was a special day; apparently they would open the coffin and allow the faithful to kiss the slippered feet of the saint and make any request they cared to. The composition of the crowd showed how well loved the saint was by the Corfiots: there were elderly peasant women in their best black clothes, and their husbands, hunched as olive-trees, with sweeping white moustaches; there were fishermen, bronzed and muscular, with the dark stains of octopus ink on their shirts; there were the sick too, the mentally defective, the consumptive, the crippled, old people who could hardly walk, and babies wrapped and bound like cocoons, their pale, waxy little faces crumpled up as they coughed and coughed. There were even a few tall, wild-looking Albanian shepherds, moustached and with shaven heads, wearing great sheepskin cloaks. This dark multi-coloured wedge of humanity moved slowly towards the dark door of the church, and we were swept along with it,

Detail of a solid silver incense burner hanging in St. Spyridon's church.

Hanging the laundry out to dry.
A colourful street scene.

Opposite page.
A secluded cove where cypress
trees grow down to the edge of
turquoise blue waters.

St. Spiridon's great silver coffin
standing upright for the
worshippers to pay their respects.

wedged like pebbles in a lava-flow. By now Margo had been pushed well ahead of me, while Mother was equally far behind. I was caught firmly between five fat peasant women, who pressed on me like cushions and exuded sweat and garlic, while Mother was hopelessly entangled between two of the enormous Albanian shepherds. Steadily, firmly, we were pushed up the steps and into the church.

Inside, it was dark as a well, lit only by a bed of candles that bloomed like yellow crocuses along one wall. A bearded, tall-hatted priest clad in black robes flapped like a crow in the gloom, making the crowd form into a single line that filed down the church, past the great silver coffin, and out through another door into the street. The coffin was standing upright, looking like a silver chrysalis, and at its lower end a portion had been removed so that the saint's feet, clad in the richly-embroidered slippers, peeped out. As each person reached the coffin he bent, kissed the feet, and murmured a prayer, while at the top of the sarcophagus the saint's black and withered face peered out of a glass panel with an expression of acute distaste. It became evident

that, whether we wanted to or not, we were going to kiss Saint Spyridon's feet. I looked back and saw Mother making frantic efforts to get to my side, but the Albanian bodyguard would not give an inch, and she struggled ineffectually. Presently she caught my eye and started to grimace and point at the coffin, shaking her head vigorously. I was greatly puzzled by this, and so were the two Albanians, who were watching her with undisguised suspicion. I think they came to the conclusion that Mother was about to have a fit, and with some justification, for she was scarlet in the face, and her grimaces were getting wilder and wilder. At last, in desperation, she threw caution to the winds and hissed at me over the heads of the crowd:

'Tell Margo . . . *not* to kiss . . . kiss the air . . . kiss the *air*.'

I turned to deliver Mother's message to Margo, but it was too late; there she was, crouched over the slippered feet, kissing them with an enthusiasm that enchanted and greatly surprised the crowd. When it came to my turn I obeyed Mother's instructions, kissing loudly and with a

considerable show of reverence a point some six inches above the saint's left foot. Then I was pushed along and disgorged through the church door and out into the street, where the crowd was breaking up into little groups, laughing and chattering. Margo was waiting on the steps, looking extremely self-satisfied. The next moment Mother appeared, shot from the door by the brawny shoulders of her shepherds. She staggered wildly down the steps and joined us.

'Those *shepherds*,' she exclaimed faintly. 'So ill-mannered . . . the smell nearly killed me . . . a mixture of incense and garlic . . . How do they manage to smell like that?'

'Oh, well,' said Margo cheerfully. 'It'll have been worth it if Saint Spyridon answers my request.'

'A most *insanitary* procedure,' said Mother, 'more likely to spread disease than cure it. I dread to think what we would have caught if we'd *really* kissed his feet.'

'But I kissed his feet,' said Margo, surprised.

'Margo! You didn't!'

'Well, everyone else was doing it.'

'And after I expressly told you *not* to.'

'You never told me not to . . .'

I interrupted and explained that I had been too late with Mother's warning.

'After all those people have been slobbering over those slippers you have to go and kiss them.'

'I was only doing what the others did.'

' I can't think what on earth possessed you to do such a thing.'

'Well, I thought he might cure my acne.'

'Acne!' said Mother scornfully. 'You'll be lucky if you don't catch something to go with the acne.'

The next day Margo went down with a severe attack of influenza, and Saint Spyridon's prestige with Mother reached rock bottom.

(My Family and Other Animals)

131

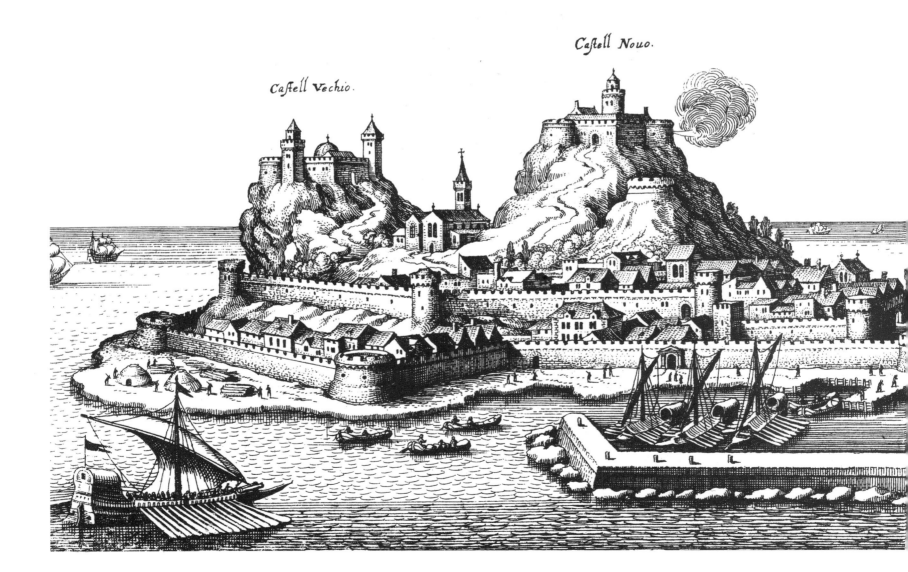

Castell Vechio.

Castell Nouo.

8 Architecture

A. Aphrodite Agoropoulou-Birbili

Where shades of Homer's Phaeacians still abound,
Where East and West embrace with lovers' sighs,
Where myriad olives wrap the cypress round,
In endless blue this emerald jewel lies.

K. Palamas, "The Quiet Life" from Motherlands.
(Translated from the Greek)

The cultural life of Corfu, the most Westernised part of Greece, blossoms against the backdrop of the island's architecture. Its buildings mirror the long process through which the island's refined society, Greek and Orthodox for the most part, followed the course of Western history for many centuries to create an environment worthy of and close to the Western spirit, yet at the same time retained a pronounced local flavour. Here the renaissance, baroque and classical repertoires came to be successfully applied to local artistic traditions.

Corfu town, the island's capital, was once completely walled and fortified. Most of its structures date from the Venetian period (1386 - 1797). Contrasting with the almost solid mass of the town's multi-storey buildings is the open area known as the Spianada or Esplanade. Together with the two Fortresses - the Old, or Byzantine, and the New - it attests to the defensive history role of the town.

In the Byzantine period, the Old Fortress and the town were one and the same. The ancient city, Chersoupolis, had been gradually deserted after a catastrophic attack by the Goths. Around the sixth century AD, the remaining inhabitants began to build their new city on the closest defensible site, the small pronged peninsula whose mediaeval name of Korypho - "summit" - provided the West with the name Corfu.

Corfu town, the island's capital, was once completely walled and fortified. Most structures date from the Venetian period, 1386-1797.

133

The 'Contra fossa', a moat of sea water divides the old fortress from the island.

The Byzantines, followed by the Despots of Epiros and then the Angevins, fortified this acropolis and built on its summit two fortresses , the Castel da Mare, Castel Vecchio, and the Castel da Terra. In their wake came the Venetians, who strengthened the mediaeval defensive core of the complex with new structures, and even divided it from the island proper by a moat of sea water, the Contrafossa, thus creating the powerful fortress which withstood the first Turkish siege of 1537.

When the increased use of artillery necessitated a new kind of fortification, the architect sent from Venice to modernise the installations was Michele Sanmicheli, one of the finest military engineers of his day. The structure he built in front of the contrafossa consisted of two large bastions named after the garrison commandants of the time, Martinengo and Savorgnan, while a majestic entrance gate was constructed between them. This work, completed in 1558, gave the Old Fortress its final shape. Equipped with casemates, barracks, storehouses, an arsenal, cisterns and many underground tunnels for communication, it became impregnable.

The area within the acropolis was limited, however, and so from quite early on a settlement began to develop outside its walls. It was known as the "outer town" *(xopoli)* or *"borgo"*, and eventually developed into a large town which,

after it was fortified towards the sixteenth century, was recognised as the island's main centre. Construction of the fortifications was entrusted to the military engineer Ferrante Vitelli, and included the defensive walls and a New Fortress (Fortezza Nuova), so called to distinguish it from the earlier one.

The Old Fortress (Fortezza Vecchia) remained chiefly a military base after the transfer of the capital, but maintained certain religious and secular buildings of which the most important was the palace of the Supervisor (or *Provveditore*), destroyed during the last World War. The buildings that survive mostly belong to the period of the British Protectorate (1814-64). Those that stand out today include the elongated barracks near the entrance, the military hospital, and the ponderous Doric order church of St George, built to the south for the British garrison.

The New Fortress, which complemented the first fortification works of the town, played only a defensive role; no civilian houses were included within the walls. The impressive main gate with its Venetian lion faces the harbour, while a second opens up to the town. Of those buildings still extant, likewise from the British period, the most impressive is the huge barracks crowning the summit which indicates that the site still had defensive significance even in the nineteenth century.

The fortress seen from a walkway leading down to the harbour.

The impressive main gate of the new fortress with its Venetian lion.

An eighteenth-century drawing of
an old cistern in the market place
which has recently been restored.

Opposite page.
A sunlit street flanked by urban
dwellings.

The original Venetian defences, with the additions made by the engineer Verneda in the seventeenth century and by Marshal von der Schulenburg in the eighteenth, together with those made by future occupants, remained untouched till 1864. When the fortresses were dismantled, as a preliminary to the fusion of the Ionian islands with the new Greek State, the town of Corfu spread unhindered beyond her old boundaries, finally merging with the suburbs that had sprung up around it during the Venetian period.

Despite damage from bombing during the Second World War, the present town has managed to preserve its character almost intact, and a sense of historical continuity pervades the entire architectural area. The mansions and austere public buildings of the Venetian period strongly influenced by Renaissance and baroque trends, combine with the simpler urban dwellings and more traditional houses of the lower classes of the town, the churches with their tall belfries, and even the neo-classical public and private buildings from the French and British period, to weave a densely structured continuous pattern that makes up an especially charming and unique whole.

The form the town took was basically defined by the narrowness of the available area and its defensive character. Both the expansive square, the Spianada, which divides the town from the Old Fortress, and the rectilinear and radial arrangement of the streets immediately behind it, owe their existence to initial defensive requirements. The same applies to the junction of the settlement's main streets with the four gates of the enclosure walls (the Porta Raimonda and Porta Reale, demolished in the nineteenth century, the Porta Spilea, and the Porta San Nicolo). In contrast, the remaining secondary streets, the *Kantounia*, are freely developed, creating a complex narrow web with stairways (*skalinades*) and vaulted passages.

Despite the initial labyrinthine impression, however, the Corfiot *Kantounia* have been flexibly adjusted to the contours of the ground surface with a pleasantly aesthetic result.

Especially interesting is the lay-out of the main streets which also serve as the town's commercial thoroughfares, such as Nicolaou Theotoki Street and Eugeniou Voulgareos Street with their characteristic covered arcades, known in Corfu as "*volta*".

A bell tower stands out strongly against the sky.

Characteristic covered arcades, known in Corfu as 'volta', form the background for a welcome cup of coffee at one of the many cafes in the Liston.

Page 140.
An unusually shaped house seen in the Kantounia, the narrow streets of the town.

Page 141.
The Ricchi family residence, with its characteristic porch and arched façade ornamented with grotesque stone faces.

The most important building in town, the Loggia dei Nobili of the seventeenth century was later converted into the Teatro San Giacomo and now serves as the Town Hall.

Opposite page. Parisian Rue de Rivoli-style lamps hang in the Liston, Corfu Town.

The network of streets is interspersed with open areas. The Spianada, a relic of the defensive needs of the past, finally became the town's main functional centre and is graced by some of the island's finest nineteenth-century buildings. In the residential areas, small squares have been left open to serve the local community, mostly in front of churches. They are usually encountered quite suddenly around a bend of one of the *candunia*, or on emerging from under one of the *volta*, as in the case of the picturesque Kremasti Square with its central feature of a well-head, reminiscent of a Venetian *campiello*. The town's main square, and the commercial and cultural centre during the Venetian period, is Platea Demarchiou, where the Town Hall stands. It used to be flanked to the west by the residence, no longer extant, of the Venetian governor, the *Bailo*. The remaining three sides include the Latin cathedral of St James (a handsome seventeenth-century building with baroque corbels adorning the roof, tower and belfry), the eighteenth-century residence of the Roman Catholic archbishop with its fine balcony and balustrade along the axis of the façade (now a branch of the Bank of Greece), and finally the most important Venetian building in the town, the Loggia Nobili of the seventeenth-century, built with blocks of local hard limestone. The simple, elegant shape

with its large arches expresses the structure's function and importance. Converted into a theatre in the eighteenth century (and named the Teatro San Giacomo after the neighbouring cathedral), it has served as the Town Hall since the early twentieth century.

Other public buildings erected during the Venetian period included a granary, an orphanage and a pawnbroker's shop (Monte di Pietá), as well as military buildings such as the Grimani barracks (also known as the Ionian Academy, because that institution, the first Greek university, was once housed there). This imposing, austere building on the southern side of the Spianada was destroyed during the last war and has only recently been reconstructed.

Corfu assumed its final form some eighty years after the construction of the town walls. The French and then the British made very few changes to the plan of the town, although they clearly left their mark on its general character. The building complex of the Spianada, with its handsome covered arcade or *volta*, known as the *"Liston"*, where the inhabitants now perform their evening promenade, is perhaps the main witness to the former presence of the French.

Handsome old town houses glimpsed through the trees.

Opposite page.
Top. Important mansions in the old town.

Bottom. View of the old town.

Stylistically, it reflects the monumental concepts of Napoleonic town planning in its uniform arrangement of rectilinear shapes, much in the manner of the Rue de Rivoli in Paris. Interestingly, the Spianada complex, part of a larger programme, was planned and partly executed by a Greek in charge of the civil engineering department, the engineer John Parmesan.

The British left a much more visible stamp on the entire town. A great many buildings, both ordinary and public, were erected during that period by gifted architects who adapted the neo-classical style to the area, breathing fresh life into the architecture of Corfu. The most important work of the period is the Georgian palace of St Michael and St George on the Spianada (built 1819 - 23), once the residence of the British Lord High Commissioners. Together with the Maitland monument, it marks a prelude to the neo-classical style in Greece. Both are the work of Colonel George Whitmore of the Royal Engineers. The façade of this monumental composition, inspired by Palladian models, exhibits a Doric colonnade punctuated by the two majestic gates of St Michael and St George; its ends curve to embrace the northern side of the square.

The important neo-classical building of the Ionian Bank, established in 1839, work of the gifted Corfiot architect John Chronis. The Bank still operates from the same building today.

Opposite page.
. .... of the palace of St. Michael and St. George framed in an archway.

Also important are the neo-classical buildings of the Ionian Bank, the Ionian Parliament, and the family residence of the first President of Greece, Count Capodistrias, which once housed the

offices of the Prefecture. The latter building, with its fine Corinthian pilasters, is considered one of the most beautiful monuments of modern Greece. All these are the work of the gifted Corfiot architect, John Chronis. Two more important nineteenth-century buildings stand outside the town. They are the neo-classical villa of Mon Repos on the Analipsis hill, and the Achilleion (see chapter 6).

Yet the most interesting architectural structures encountered in the town of Corfu are the multi-storeyed town houses, divided into apartments. The limited area available to the inhabitants combined with the density of the population dictated the need for this design long before it became widespread architectural practice. The houses of the Venetian period were three or four floors high, but the successive additions they have undergone provide a yardstick for the growing pressure on living space over time. Normally they were built on small plots with almost 95 per cent structural cover; narrow air vents, the so-called *kanizelles* extended from one end of the block to the other.

The houses of the British period at times cover a broader surface area by using more than one plot, and are often six or seven storeys high. The Venetian houses, which for the most part are identical, are reminiscent of those in Venice or Naples, with their regular rows of windows, lower arcades, stone balconies, railings, finely fashioned corbels provided with a hole for washing lines or used to support window sills, heraldic devices, and beautiful doorways (the *portonia*), all usually complemented by colours of red or ochre on the external wall surfaces, contrasting with the carved frames and green embrasures.

All these features play a basic role in defining the nature of the architectural style and may be said to stem from Western influence. But the tradition of the popular craftsman is also important in that he remodels features borrowed from the West to blend in with the island's surroundings and the mentality of the inhabitants. The more recent buildings of the British period, influenced to an extent by the classicist school, are characterised by a symmetry and austerity in the arrangement of their piecemeal elements and are often adorned with balconies whose variation from floor to floor provide the building with a feeling of movement and variety.

View of the Giallinas residence, as
seen from the esplanade.

The town's mansions are likewise of architectural interest, as are the villas in the countryside (see chapter 5). Of the mansions, typical examples are the Giallinas and Ricchi residences. Their initial form has changed with time, of course, but the façade with its characteristic porch is still preserved in both.

Contrasting with the town's Renaissance - or baroque - inspired buildings are the more humble village dwellings where Western influence is far less apparent and that of the local popular tradition more prominent in the new scale and mass which now correspond to the everyday needs of the Corfiot farmer. As a rule these are two-storey structures with the living quarters on the upper floor and ancillary areas below. The stables are usually located in another building. The simplest ground plan consists of a single room, while more developed types have more rooms, symmetrically gathered around a central area opening out on both sides, a style

Opposite page.
In the foreground, the town house
of the celebrated Corfiot artist
Giallinas, and in the background
the old Flamburiari mansion, now
the Cavalieri Hotel.

reminiscent of the arrangement of mansions in both town and countryside. Internally, the village house is simple and unadorned, with very little furniture. The only real necessities are a high bed with its storage area below, and a carved or painted wooden clothes-chest.

The oldest examples of these buildings are in the shape of a simple cube with a steep interior wooden staircase leading from the lower to the upper floor by means of a trap-door, an indication of the insecurity of the period. The more recent buildings have an external stone staircase with a masonry balustrade usually terminating in a covered landing on the first floor. Under this landing we find the arched entrance to the ground floor. These features were undoubtedly added in more peaceful times. Both the exterior stairway and the portico usually found on the ground or upper floor vary greatly in type and are of particular architectural interest.

In contrast to the town's renaissance or baroque inspired buildings are the more humble village abodes.

Porticos vary greatly and are of particular architectural interest, especially those found in the country.

Village houses are simple and unadorned in contrast to those in town. The oldest examples are built in the shape of a cube.

Ecclesiastical architecture on Corfu conforms with that in the rest of the Ionian Islands. With only the minimum of examples from the Byzantine period on the island, thanks to the long period of Frankish rule, the inhabitants built their churches according to Western architectural styles without diminishing their steadfast devotion to the Orthodox faith.

The first Christian structures are mainly represented by the ruins of the Early Christian basilica of Paleopolis, built during the fifth century by Bishop Jovian with material taken from ancient monuments of the area. The church of Saints Jason and Sosipatros, dating from the tenth century, represents the only Byzantine monument of the domed inscribed-cross type on the island.

The remaining Corfiot churches are as a rule built either with a single aisle, or much more rarely in a form of a three-aisled timber-roofed basilica; they belong mostly to the Venetian period. A low narthex often surrounds two or three sides of the town churches. Next to the church and sometimes on top of it, may stand the house of the priest - yet a further indication of the scarcity of space. Exteriors are usually relatively simple and austere. They may be decorated with relief doorways bearing Renaissance or baroque formal features, and large arched windows. The churches' most typical features are the tall belfries, sometimes built as towers, sometimes in the form of a perforated wall framed by corbels.

While the exterior surfaces may be plain, the church interiors are richly decorated. The masonry iconostasis screen, the portable icons, the painted decoration of the ceiling, the wood-carved pews, the candle-holders and various votive offerings all go to create a profoundly reverent atmosphere.

A church at Nifes.

Opposite page.
Interior of the Byzantine church of
Saints Jason and Sosipatros which
represents the only Byzantine
monument of the domed inscribed
cross type on the island.

The gallery is always to the west, while the entrances are protected from the wind by a wooden swing-door. Western elements can be found in the ciborium over the altar and the kneeling stools to the right and left of the templon. The church housing the relics of St Spyridon, the island's patron saint, is undoubtedly the most famous on Corfu and was built in 1590 to replace a previous church destroyed during the construction of the town walls. Its immensely tall belfry dominates the town and recalls its near contemporary, that of S. Giorgio dei Greci in Venice. The ceiling decoration was painted in the eighteenth century by the eminent icon-painter, Panayotis Doxaras, but his work was destroyed and only a modern reproduction can be seen today.

Other examples of architectural interest in the town are the churches of the Virgin Antivouniotissa and of St John, which preserve their surrounding narthexes; that of St Andrew, appended to a three-storey structure; and the only two extant three-aisled churches, the cathedral and the church of the Virgin, Panayia Ton Xenon. A few Latin churches still survive.

Apart from the Duomo, the *katholikon* of the old monastery of St Francis can still be seen, as can the Virgin of Tenedos, perhaps the most important from an architectural perspective thanks to its Renaissance-style dome covering the altar area, reminiscent of the Duomo of Florence. Even the tower-like belfry from the old Annunziata still exists.

The monasteries of Corfu do not as a rule follow the procedures of the Byzantine rite but allow for a free development of the courtyard, just as Latin monasteries do. Not far from the town lies the historic monastery of the Virgin Platytera, restored after its destruction by the French, and the resting place of Count Capodistrias. The *katholikon* of the monastery of the Saints Theodore, which is located on the site of Paleopolis, incorporates part of an Early Christian basilica. The arrangement of the cells in the neighbouring monastery of St Euphemia is especially picturesque. Both these monasteries are of special interest due to the arrangement of their structural features. Last but not least, the Paleokastritsa monastery overlooks one of the most beautiful sites on the island.

*The Catholic Cathedral of
St. James, a fine 17th-century
building with baroque corbels
adorning the roof, the tower and
the belfry.*

9 Art and Artists

Evita Arapoglou

It was after the fall of Crete to the Turks in 1669 that a great number of Greek artists and craftsmen sought refuge in the Ionian Islands. Crete, under Venetian rule since the thirteenth century, had attracted the majority of Greek Orthodox artists forced to flee from Constantinople, the capital of the Byzantine Empire, after it fell to the Ottomans in 1453. The Paleologian iconographical tradition was thus transferred not only to isolated monastic centres such as Mount Athos or Meteora, but also to wealthy commercial centres, primarily Crete, which under the tolerant Venetian administrative system offered more attractive prospects to migrating artists seeking a new place to settle and practise their skill. Artistic activity in Crete

during the sixteenth and seventeenth centuries was significant enough to give rise to the so-called Cretan School of painting. It was based on the Byzantine model: precise outlines of forms, firm geometrical rendering of draperies and austere representation of facial expression - features that characterise both the numerous icon panels and the mural decorations in local churches.

These centuries had seen a constant expansion of communications between Crete and other territories under Venetian control, such as the Ionian Islands. The numerous artists who travelled to Venice in order to study or work often spent time in the Ionian Islands - mostly

Oil painting of Corfu by Haralambos Pachis (1844-1891) showing the fortress and the villa of 'Mon Repos', built for the British High Commissioner. (53 x 75 cm). Koutlides collection, Athens.

Opposite page. A charming study of a Corfiot woman, the work of Constantine Iatras (1822-1880), oil on canvas, 100 x 75 cm, now in the Koutlides collection.

Zakinthos and Corfu - which lay on their route. Works of high quality were increasingly sought after, while artists with established reputations signed and dated works that clearly display a gradual harmonious adaptation of Venetian Renaissance trends to the Byzantine tradition.

Michael Damaskinos, Father Emmanuel Tzanes and Theodoros Poulakis, are a few of the important representatives of the Cretan School whose work was related to the Ionian Islands and Corfu in particular. Damaskinos must have worked in Corfu around 1571, and a number of his works can be seen on the screen of the church of the Resurrection in the Municipal Cemetery and in the cathedral of Christ Pantocrator. Icons by Tzanes, a prolific religious painter who spent ten years in Corfu before his appointment in 1659 as parish priest to the Orthodox church of Saint George in Venice, belong to the church of Saints Jason and Sosipatros, the church of Panayia Ton Xenon, and the monastery of Platytera. Poulakis worked extensively in Venice before he settled in Corfu in 1675. Until his death in 1692 he produced works highly influenced by Venetian painting, some of them preserved in the monasteries of Platytera and Paleokastritsa.

Artistic commerce flourished throughout the Venetian communities, especially after the introduction of the popular portable icons. Merchants and members of the Ionian Islands' aristocracy commissioned Cretan masters to paint devotional icons. (Damaskinos' Saint John the Baptist, originally in the church of St Spyridon Flamburiari and now in Zakinthos Museum, is an example of masterly sixteenth-century iconography.) To these were added a large number of icons, ecclesiastical objects and treasures from Cretan churches which were rescued by migrating Cretan artists during the conquest of Crete and subsequently dedicated to churches in the Ionian Islands.

While the post-Byzantine tradition spread through the islands, some distinct signs of Western European culture were also appearing. Italian works of art adorned some Orthodox churches, religious etchings by Italian artists appeared in icon niches - *iconostasia* - and houses were described as being decorated in Italian style. The Treaty of Karlowitz in 1699 reconfirmed the Venetian domination over the islands and consequently reinforced the cultural

links with Venice, where throughout the eighteenth century artists would continue to study not just religious but also secular painting. That century was characterised in the islands by a complete turn towards the West and a break with Byzantine ideas. Pictorial space was treated in Italian High Renaissance aesthetic terms, plasticity and three-dimensional perception became the essential aims to be achieved in compositions that remained primarily religious in subject matter.

Throughout the eighteenth century the centre of artistic activity for the Ionian Islands was probably Zakinthos. However, since Corfu was the most populous among the islands and, more importantly, their administrative and military centre, it offered some of the most prestigious commissions. Every famous artist active in the islands would visit and work in Corfu at some point during his career. The decoration of the dome of the church of Saint Spyridon in Corfu, for instance, was entrusted in 1727 to Panayotis Doxaras (1662 - 1729), a celebrated painter considered to be the founder of the school based on Western European artistic principles. This monumental project (which was unfortunately destroyed, to be restored in 1897 by copies of the original works by a later painter, Aspiotis) was described as the culmination of the Ouranies - grandiose celestial representations - that decorated the domes of newly built churches in the islands.

Doxaras, the son of a knight from Mani, had left his homeland after its occupation by the Turks and settled in the Ionian Islands. Such was his enthusiasm to explore and demonstrate the greatness of Western European painting that he translated the key treatises on painting by Leone Battista Alberti and Leonardo da Vinci into Greek. In 1726 he wrote his own manual on painting, in which he opposed the Byzantine painterly tradition and the austere conventional manner in which figures were portrayed, suggesting freer drawing from nature, anatomical studies, and naturalistic rendering of light and movement.

Focusing on the Venetian masters of the Renaissance, he explored new oil-painting techniques, thus further underlining the contrast with previous Byzantine panel techniques.

Michael Damaskinos,
Saints Sergius, Bacchus and
Justina, after 1571, 112 x 119cms,
Corfu - Museum of
Antivouniotissa.

Portraiture became very popular in the Ionian Islands during the eighteenth century. A community so economically prosperous and yet socially closed within a hierarchical structure was bound to influence the subject matter of arts, and a number of painters were commissioned to produce formal, rather stiff portraits of members of the local aristocracy, wealthy merchants, intellectuals and clergymen. Doxaras and his son Nikolaos were the official portrait-painters. Their work was characterised by particular attention to detail and was reminiscent of early Venetian Renaissance portraiture. The 1725 portrait by P. Doxaras of the Saxon Count von der Schulenburg, the Venetian general who repulsed the Turkish siege of Corfu in 1716, is among the early examples of eighteenth-century portraiture in the island.

The Italianising movement introduced by Doxaras attracted many followers. Georgios Chrysoloras (active 1730 - 47) also worked in Corfu in the Italian tradition. His works can be found in the church of Saint Eleftherios (scenes from the New Testament), in the churches of St John the Baptist at the Cisterns and Saint Varvaros at Potamos and elsewhere. Spyridon Sperantzas (active 1740 - 77) produced a host of works that decorate churches in Corfu such as Kremasti and Holy Trinity in Garitsa, and amply reflect his gradual development towards Western artistic perception. Spyridon Ventouras (1761 - 1835) from Lefkas, trained in Venice, painted the ceiling of the monastery church of Platytera. Father Nicholas Koutouzis (1741 - 1813), an eccentric priest from Zakinthos and a student of Doxaras and allegedly of Tiepolo, pursued the Renaissance ideals of the Italians and painted emotionally dramatic religious works and a great number of portraits. His works in Corfu include the dome in the church of Panayia Ton Xenon and the portrait of Governor Andrea Dona. Father Nikolaos Candounis (1767 - 1834), almost a self-taught painter, spent all his life in the Ionian Islands, where apart from his important religious works he proved a significant portrait painter of the local aristocracy and clergy of the early nineteenth century. Although most of his works were created in Zakinthos, two large and well finished compositions, The Last Supper and The Washing of Feet, were painted for the monastery of Platytera in Corfu.

Doxaras and his school may have inaugurated the formal shift towards Western European painting, but their approach to Italian artistic culture was somewhat out-dated. Since the styles they were influenced by had already faded in Italy, the artistic preferences developing in the Ionian Islands gradually changed. The message from the classicism prevailing in Western Europe was transmitted through the painter and sculptor Pavlos Prosalentis (1784 - 1837). Born in Corfu to a noble family of Byzantine origin, he studied in Rome together with his contemporary Dimitris Trivolis-Pierris (1785 - 1809) - at the Academy of St Luke. Canova's teaching and work were decisive in his development both in painting and in sculpture. He returned to his home island in 1806 and was appointed professor of sculpture in the public School of Arts which two years later became part of the Ionian Academy. During his time, drawing was included in courses offered in secondary schools, while at the Academy it complemented subjects such as philosophy and literature.

Statue by Pavlos Prosalentis of Sir Frederick Adam in front of the palace of St. Michael and St. George.

Prosalentis initially supported the Academy's pursuits but, concerned with the instability caused by contemporary political and social changes in the islands, he left for another long visit to Italy and Europe. Upon his return to Corfu he founded his successful private art school, where he taught painting and sculpture. Records state that approximately one hundred students attended during the first three years. The school was converted by the British into a Public Academy of Fine Arts, as a sign of approval of Prosalentis' work. Transferred to a Franciscan monastery, it was directed by Prosalentis, but prominent artists like the Cephalonians Gerassimos Pitzamanos and Dimitris Veghias taught architecture and painting. The curriculum concentrated on classical principles of drawing, while teaching and practice were based on casts from classical reliefs and statues.

An idyllic Corfiot scene engraved by Joseph Cartwright (38 x 63 cm). Private collection.

Prosalentis' experience abroad, as well as his understanding of neo-classicism, a style favoured by the British, made him the ideal contender for public commissions. Throughout his productive career (though few of his works have survived) he made various bronze busts (Sir Thomas Maitland, 1819, in the Senate room in the Palace) and bronze statues (Sir Frederick Adam, 1831, in front of the palace of St Michael and St George), as well as decorative reliefs for the Palace. He also organised a museum based on his family collection of antiquities and ancient coins. In 1820 he received from the Ionian Government the Order of St Michael and St George in recognition of his contribution to the cultural development of the island. Prosalentis was instrumental in founding through his teaching a basis for understanding Greek classical heritage. His death in 1837 resulted in the decline of the school, as there was no direct continuation of his work in the Ionian Islands, although the pursuit of neo - classical principles and the appreciation of the Hellenic heritage was to characterise every artistic endeavour in independent Greece throughout the nineteenth century.

It was during that century, with its wave of learned admiration for the Hellenic world, that the greatest number of West European traveller artists visited Corfu. The pilgrimage to the sites of classical antiquities fired the imagination of a number of painters travelling to explore the aesthetics of an idealised world. Especially in the case of those arriving from France and Italy, the long voyage usually began with the Ionian Islands and then continued to the Peloponnese, Athens and the mainland, and the islands of the Aegean, and often reached the coast of Asia Minor and Constantinople. Corfu, with the comforts it offered, seemed the ideal introduction to the land of Greece. Travellers were captivated by the natural beauty of the island - its dramatic contrasts, overgrown gardens, spectacular cliffs, distant hillside villages, or picturesque coastline reflected in the still Ionian Sea. Both their sketchbooks and formal paintings and water-colours abound with views of the island's idyllic countryside pictured against Albanian mountains covered with snow - all

these works reflecting the Romantic vision through which Western Europe tended to perceive the Hellenic world.

Hugh William Williams (1773 - 1829) visited the Ionian Islands in 1817, and his watercolour views were exhibited in Edinburgh five years later. William Page (1794 - 1879) was also inspired by Corfu's landscape beauty around the same time. Joseph Schranz, a Maltese artist, probably visited the islands during the mid-1830s, en route to Crete. John Frederick Lewis (1805 - 76) painted views of Corfu in 1840. Edward Lear (1812 - 88), whose vision of Corfu is discussed in another chapter of this book, was probably the most prolific British painter of nineteenth-century Greece. The most popular theme that inspired these and other traveller artists was the town of Corfu, with its imposing citadel seen from a distance and its expanse of lush green landscape to provide a dramatic framing of the subject. Here were the elements of an ideal composition for a nineteenth-century romantic landscape painter.

View of the old fortress from
the bay of Garitsa.
Watercolour by Angelos Giallinas
(40 x 74 cm).
Private collection.

Joseph Cartwright (1789 - 1829), Paymaster General to the British Garrison at Corfu between 1816 and 1820, was one of the most important illustrators of the island's life and countryside. In 1821 he published his *Views of the Ionian Islands* and in 1822 his *Selections of the Costume of Albania and Greece.* His many water-colours depict architectural monuments set in the beauty of the countryside as well as scenes from the island's customs. The *Procession of Saint Spyridon,* among the most interesting and characteristic of his works, was probably inspired by the traditional Venetian compositions of religious processions also painted by artists of the Ionian Islands such as Koutouzis and Candounis.

This ceremonial representation of the community's eccesiastical custom was seen in "From the street of St Basil from the Esplanade to Corfu" where the buildings in the foreground are to the south-east of the church of St Spyridon, the home of the relic of the saint. The grand procession, attended by all members of

the community, clad in the festive costumes honouring the importance of the occasion, is pictured in fascinating detail.

In 1862, two years before unification with the independent state of Greece, Corfu participated in the International Exhibition in London, with paintings by Prosalentis and by some British military artists. Despite the rather uneventful period after Prosalentis, the island continued to be an artistic centre. However, it was the new generation of Corfiot artists such as Pachis, younger members of the Prosalentis family, Bokatsiambis, Giallinas, Samartzis and Scarvellis, who created a fresh artistic atmosphere. Their frequent contact with Athens and its School of Fine Arts prompted a new direction in the development of painting. With the exception of Pachis and Samartzis, who spent most of their life in Corfu, these artists made regular returns to the island, drawing inspiration and deriving influences from the various places they had travelled to and worked in.

163

Vikentios Bokatsiambis (1856-1932), Corfiot Woman in costume from Potamos, *watercolour, 24 x 14 cm, Averoff Collection (no. 53), Metsovo.*

Charalambos Pachis (1844 - 91) studied in Naples and Rome, where he became influenced by the prevailing bright, rather decorative style. Returning to Corfu in 1870, he founded a private school of painting which was to be attended by many future artists of the Ionian Islands. He painted religious compositions (some for the screen of Saint Spyridon), historical scenes (especially from the Greek War of Independence) and genre themes, though perhaps his most successful works are his compositions inspired by local traditions and festivities. His painting *Celebrating the First of May in Corfu* is characteristic of his style - full of decorative detail and vividly reproducing the event's joyful atmosphere. Corfiot men sing and play musical instruments in a central market street of Corfu town, one of them holding a cypress tree decorated with festive ribbons, the symbol from an old custom. The painting is characteristic of his very effective use of flatly painted luminous surfaces interrupted by abrupt geometrical shadows. (See p. 182)

Vikentios Bokatsiambis (1856 - 1932), a Corfiot artist of aristocratic origin, studied in Marseille and at the Academy of St Luke in Rome. His ties with the Italian artistic style dominated his work after his return to Corfu in 1895. From 1900 he was based in Athens, where he worked and taught for many years; but he regularly visited Corfu, where he painted numerous landscape views and portraits of Corfiots in their local costume. He worked primarily in watercolour, and his compositions are reminiscent of the Italian impressionist school where a mosaic of freely-applied small brushstrokes characteristically reproduce romanticised detailed pictures.

Angelos Giallinas (1857 - 1939), the most celebrated Greek watercolourist, produced some masterly delicate interpretations of his island's scenery. An apprentice of Pachis, he pursued his studies in Venice and Rome, and settled back in Corfu in 1877. At the time of his first exhibition in Athens in 1886, he met the British Ambassador Ford, who commissioned him to paint a series of watercolours with views of Venice, Corfu and Spain. He travelled extensively in Europe, painting and exhibiting mainly watercolour views; among his most famous are his views of Athens and the classical monuments, and of Constantinople, but his Corfu landscapes remain paramount in his *oeuvre*. His eloquent brushstrokes convey translucent images of the island's misty serenity, while his unique sensitivity to the variations of light responds to the characteristic stillness of the Ionian Sea. His seascapes and views of markets, little secret alleys or abundant gardens, were very popular during his life, and many of his works are kept in his house in Corfu. In 1902 he founded the Art School of Corfu, and in 1907 - 8 he was in charge of the mural decoration of the Achilleion, the villa built by Elisabeth, Empress of Austria.

Angelos Giallinas (1857-1939),
Garden in Corfu,
watercolour, 39 x 72 cm,
Averoff Collection (no 82),
Metsovo.

Angelos Giallinas (1857-1939),
Alley in Corfu,
watercolour, 31 x 16 cm,
Averoff Collection (no 83),
Metsovo.

Angelos Giallinas (1857-1939),
Greengrocer in Corfu,
watercolour, 32 x 16 cm,
Averoff Collection (no 84),
Metsovo.

Spyridon Scarvellis (1868-1942),
View of the Castello,
watercolour, 31 x 46 cm,
Leventis Collection, Athens.

Markos Zavitsianos (1884-1923),
View of Corfu,
etching, 8 x 13 cm,
National Gallery, Athens.

Markos Zavitsianos (1884-1923),
Peasants of Corfu,
etching, 8 x 11 cm,
National Gallery, Athens.

Pericles Tsirigotis (1865 - 1924) and Georgios Samartzis (1868 - 1925) were Corfiot painters also inspired by themes from their island, particularly portraits and landscapes. Spyridon Scarvellis (1868 - 1942) studied in Trieste and Rome, and painted vivid and picturesque watercolour views of Corfu while being involved in various decorative projects such as the decoration of the Achilleion. Markos Pierris (1865 - 1954) studied at the Academy of St Luke in Rome and returned to Corfu to become a proficient landscape and portrait painter using mainly watercolour and pastels in a rather Italian style. Lykourgos Kogevinas (1884 - 1940) studied in Paris between 1905 and 1908 at the Grande Chaumière and at the Académie Julien. Although he spent most of his life between Paris and Athens, Corfiot themes frequently feature in his work.

Markos Zavitsianos (1883 - 1944), born in Constantinople to a family of Corfiot origin, settled in Corfu in 1902. After studying in Munich and Paris, he returned in 1909 to Corfu, where he illustrated periodicals and proved an excellent printmaker, especially working from his etchings. He was mostly inspired by scenes from everyday Corfiot life and characteristically detailed landscape views.

Perhaps the last and most famous artist who worked exclusively in Corfu was the painter and printmaker Nikos Ventouras (1899 - 1990), born in the island and a student of Giallinas. He painted scenes inspired by the countryside and history of Corfu. After 1932 he became increasingly involved with printmaking techniques. Considered a leading printmaker in twentieth-century Greece, he left a vast number of prints - his etchings were among his most characteristic - reflecting his love for the Corfiot life and countryside, equally apparent in his early figurative as well as his later abstract expressionistic style.

But Corfu has never ceased to attract artists throughout our century. Some of the best known pictures inspired by the island were painted by Constantinos Parthenis (1878 - 1967). Before he settled in Athens and became one of his country's most influential modern artists, he lived in Corfu between 1912 and 1917, together with Angelos Giallinas and Nikolaos Lytras. His compositions are bright landscape views, often focusing on the abundant pine-trees, depicted with his characteristic bold shapes and colours. Nikos Hadjikyriakos-Ghika, one of the leading figures in twentieth-century Greek painting, made regular visits to Corfu during the seventies and eighties, producing images inspired by the exuberant dense greenery of the Mediterranean countryside. His pictures of olive-groves, trees and shrubs, as well as of his magnificent Corfu house with its surroundings, are eloquent of the aesthetic magnetism that the island has never ceased to exert on the artist's inspiration.

Nikos Ventouras (1899-1990),
Church of Saint Spyridon,
1949, lithograph on stone,
29 x 21 cm,
National Gallery, Athens.

Constantinos Parthenis (1878-1967),
Pine Trees in Corfu,
c. 1918, oil on canvas,
90 x 96 cm,
National Gallery, Athens.

Opposite page top.
Constantinos Parthenis (1878-1967),
Castello Mibelli,
oil, 24 x 33 cm,
M. Apergis Collection, Athens.

Nikos Ghika (1906-),
Olive Trees in Corfu,
1978, coloured pencils,
Ghika Museum, Athens.

Opposite page bottom.
Edward Lear (1812-1888),
The Citadel, Corfu.
Pencil, pen and ink, 18.1 x 41.3 cm.
Dated 11.00 am February 6, 1856.
Private collection.
By kind permission of
The Fine Art Society.

Vassilios Hatzis (1870-1915)
Morning in Corfu,
oil on canvas, 70 x 120 cm,
Koutlides Collection, Athens.

Edward Lear (1812-1888),
Corfu and the Albanian Mountains.
Oil on canvas, 34x55cm
Signed with monogram.
By kind permission of
Pyms Gallery, London.

10 Edward Lear

Peter Nahum

**The Owl and the Pussy-cat went to sea
In a beautiful pea-green boat,
They took some honey, and plenty of money,
Wrapped up in a five-pound note.**

Edward Lear was the most talented and evocative topographical painter of his generation, but history is not always kind to its most gifted forefathers. During his lifetime, and until recently, he was recognized by all but a few as the man who wrote nonsense rhymes, and hailed as the inventor of the "Limerick" (a word he never used himself). For the greater part of this century collectors prized his watercolours but dismissed his oil paintings. Today, most know his nonsense song "The Owl and the Pussy Cat", although few would identify him as the author.

Born into a middle-class family in 1812, Edward Lear was the twentieth of twenty-one children. When he was four his mother, no longer able to cope, handed him over to his eldest sister Ann to bring up. She encouraged him in artistic studies and he became, without training, a talented artist, undertaking his first commissions at the age of fifteen. He wrote poetry and had a good musical ear, setting verses to music and accompanying them on the piano, both publicly and as an after-dinner entertainment. At the age of sixteen Edward collaborated on illustrating the book, *Illustrations of Ornithology*. By the age of twenty he had become an associate member of the Linnean Society, had been commissioned by Lord Stanley to draw the birds and animals in his menagerie, and had published his now famous lithographs of the parrot family.

*Potamos, Corfu.
Watercolour by Edward Lear from
the collection of
The Hon. Sir Steven Runciman CH,
by kind permission of National
Gallery of Scotland.*

All this seems an easy and brilliant start to a young man's career. However, Lear's genius, like so many others', had grown from adversity. Although he lived in his parents' crowded and noisy house, it was clear that they had never wanted him. He was lovingly brought up by his sister, but felt a strong sense of rejection. The young Edward suffered from a terrifying and frightening disease: a violent form of epilepsy combined with bouts of severe depression. These depressive attacks and incessant seizures were to affect him for the rest of his life. Epilepsy was perceived at that time as an untreatable mental illness. It left its sufferers not only with a strong sense of fear but also with a deep underlying shame.

Edward Lear became one of the great travellers of the nineteenth century, often enduring exacting hardships to reach his goals. He was a terrible sailor, suffering discomfort and seasickness. He was driven to search out peaceful and secluded places, escaping the memories of the noisy and argumentative household of his childhood and hiding the distressing symptoms of his epilepsy. His travels started when he was twenty, and by the age of twenty-five, in 1838, he had settled in Rome, where he was to stay for the next seven years. In 1848 he set off on his first journey away from mainland Europe, visiting the Mediterranean, its islands and far-flung shores. The first island he set foot on was Malta, that dry barren rock close to the African continent. Its lack of greenery could not have provided a greater contrast to his next port of call. Four days later, at three in the morning, he arrived at Corfu.

He immediately wrote to his sister Ann:

I wish I could give you an idea of the beauty of this island - it really is a paradise . . . The chief charm is the great variety of the scenery, and the extreme greenness of every place. Such magnificent groves of olives I never saw - they are gigantic. The people are a most quiet harmless race - and exceedingly civil. The Albanian shepherds in their beautiful dress are very striking.

And so began, during this brief five week visit, Lear's lifelong love affair with the Island of Corfu. Continuing his journey through Greece, Albania and Egypt, he sketched the magnificent topographical views he sought out. He had developed a unique calligraphic line (almost a shorthand in its simplicity) to describe the lie of the landscape. These drawings were usually washed in with watercolour and notated with extensive *aides-mémoire* of colours, each then

being carefully inscribed with the location, date and time of day. He would also make finished watercolours, such as the little circular view of the Citadel in Corfu that he painted on his very first day on the island.

Very much at home with watercolour, Edward Lear was, however, uneasy painting in oils. Like many inexperienced in that medium he lacked the courage to use bright colours. His palette was unadventurous and he emulated the conventions of the British provincial landscape school, using tones of brown and muddy green - those of a dreary English evening.

His ambition to exhibit at the Royal Academy, and his need to earn the far greater sums that he could command from oil painting, led him, on his return in 1850, to attend the Royal Academy Schools. He left within a year. In the summer of 1852 he was introduced to the young Pre-Raphaelite artist William Holman Hunt, fifteen years his junior. Lear was forty, and characteristically not in the slightest humiliated to ask Hunt for painting lessons. The Pre-Raphaelites, painting directly from nature, had developed new techniques to lay bright jewel-like colours onto their canvases. Lear, in contrast, worked up his oils in his studio. Under Holman Hunt's tuition Lear, released from his previous inhibitions, was able to record the subtle changes of the seductive Mediterranean light.

In Egypt, following his first visit to Corfu, Lear met Franklin Lushington, a classics scholar from Cambridge. They became great friends and for Lear, who was always cautiously independent, this friendship became the most important of his life. In 1855 Franklin Lushington was offered the post of Judge to the Supreme Court of Justice in the Ionian Islands. He would live in Corfu. This was the perfect excuse for Lear to return to the island that had made such a deep impression on him seven years before. Here, over the next twenty-two years, he would spend many of the happiest moments of his life. By the time of his death in 1888, Lear would have visited the island nine times, staying there a total of three years and four months.

Edward Lear wrote copious letters to his sister and friends recounting his experiences and describing the scenery of the island. These portrayals were, of course, those of a landscape

artist - painting colour and light with words. They serve today as a fascinating nineteenth-century travel guide. The following are some of his descriptions of the land and seascape of Corfu, grouped under geographical headings.

General

First impressions, 1848

About 3 this morning we anchored in the beautiful paradise of Corfu bay . . . The city was Venetian until 1780, but has little to recommend it - narrow streets and poky houses. But nearest the sea, there is the most beautiful esplanade in the world (on the corner of which I now look). On the farther side of this is the magnificent Palace of the Viceroy (now Lord Seaton) and beyond is the double-crowned Citadel - very picturesque . . . The women wear duck, black or blue, with a red handkerchief about their head; the men, the lower orders that is, mostly red caps, and duck full Turkish trousers. Here and there you see an Albanian all red and white, with a full petticoat like a doll's, and a sheepskin over his shoulder. Then you meet some of the priests who wear flowing black robes and beards. Mixed with them are the English soldiers and naval officers, and the upper class of Corfiotes who dress as we do; so the mixture is very picturesque . . . Afterwards I drew, drew, drew the sadly receding Corfu. Walked about deck till nearly 9. Sea quite calm.

A growing affection

Yet the more I see of this place, so the more I feel that no other spot on earth can be so full of beauty, and of variety of beauty. For you may pass your days by gigantic cliffs with breaking foam-waves below them (as at Palaiokastritsa), or on hills which overlook long seas of foliage backed by snow-covered mountain ridges (as at Garouna or Gastouri), or beneath vast olive over-branching dells full of ferns and myrtles and soft green fields of bright grass, or in gardens dark with orange and lemon groves, their fruit sparkling golden and yellow against the purple sea and the amethyst hills, or by a calm sandy shore by aloe-grown heights, rippling-sparkling curves of sea sounding gently around all day long.

The North

Horoepiskopi

I think it highly probable that you will not be able (all at once at least) to pronounce the address of the place from which I write this; so you had better call it Hokus Pokus at once, as all the English do here . . . The village is on a double rocky hill in the midst of a valley entirely full of splendid oranges and cypresses, just as if it were in a basin; on the other side of the basin are several other villages, and to the north all the hills slope away to the sea, beyond which my old friends the Khimariote mountains are seen.

Nifes

Nifes is a larger place than Hokus Pokus, but more remote, and more dirty though more picturesque. There is a quiet valley below it, almost as good as Italy, and from the high parts of the ground you look over innumerable olives to the distant sea, where Farno and the little isles lie very prettily at sunset.

Palaiokastritsa

In this procession [Palm Sunday, the Procession of St Spyridon] they use enormous candles, perhaps two feet round in size, and 12 or 14 feet long, and the effect of all this bright colour against the blue hills I thought was very nice . . .

How glorious was that blue level of sea! And the [Holm Oak] and salvia, and the white butterflies - a quiet of bygone days . . .

Panteleimona

A vast gray gray gray delicate myriads landscape, but immensely inferior to the more central views . . . O asphodels! O olives! O shadows!

Mount San Salvador

Clearer - but all the Corfu hills thick with white snow: Aghii Deka and Salvador covered . . . And Salvador, all dark purple and bright white with a long cloud, to all along the marsh road, how cold and beautiful! Khimariotes plodding along to their adopted olive homes.

Certainly it is not possible to see in all this world aught more lovely than San Salvador from 3 to 4 - peach blossom and blue and pink rose, and somewhat like a form of velvet covered hill.

Smakieras

. . . should I write on Corfu - is the improper name of one of the towns - "smack-your-arse" . . . What could a decent man do with such nomenclature?

The Centre

Afra (Alepou,Afra, Kourkoumeli and the Gouvia road)

What can be lovelier than these village scenes about Afra? - or the olive woods beyond, the bright gray and pale yellow lichen'd trunx showing out from the dark glens of foliage, here and there broken by bright green, with long streams of shadow. And the silver-edged - as it were - ever-moving sheep. The anemones, and myrtle. Ahi!

Analipsis

How beautiful is that village of Analipsis, with its scattered sheep and lambs, and the little cottages, with kids and calfs round the door . . .

In one minute I am within all those fine olive walks you have heard so much of. I have some idea of devoting a good bit of time to illustrating this little promontory, for it is full of interest, as the old city of Analipsis was built on it, and ancient coins and marbles are still found.

The corn has been cut a month past. All that was so beautifully green till June is now all pale yellow and parched dry, even under the olive, near the city, where the trees give but little shade; I have not been at Viros lately to see if the fern is green yet. All about here the ground won't leave off bursting into flowers as far as it can, and a vast crop of yellow thistles has just come out, which certainly don't give a cooler effect to the landscape, but the yellow ground contrasted with the blue and purple hills and sea is very beautiful and I do not know what season to paint in my large picture - green or yellow . . . Did I tell you of the bright blue thistles? Out of spite because she has got so few flowers, Mrs Nature has turned out one sort of thistle brilliant blue-leaves, stalks, and all - and they look like bright blue flowers at a distance.

Walked back along the Analipsis peninsula. What wonderful effects: dark blue gray filmy dells, with bright bits of gray light in olive branches here and there. After such evenings in Corfu what is left as to beauty of outer life?

Gastouri

View from the Benitses Road.

This is one of the loveliest views on the island, and is distant about six miles from the City. The beautiful slopes of olive wood seem to end in the church-crowned Promontory of Ascension; but this is not the case, as the lake of Calichiopulo is between the end of the "One-Gun Battery" road and the olive slopes. Its entrance, however, is hidden, as is one of the little island monasteries, only the "Ship of Ulysses" being visible. The citadel, the town of Corfu, Vido, and (separated by the Channel) the Mount of San Salvador, the Santa Quaranta hills, and those of Butrinto, are all beyond. Again, the landscape is finished by the many-pointed Mount Lykursi, the Pass of Gardiki and the long chain of heights thence to the range immediately above Delvino.

Edward Lear, Nifes, 1863, pencil, sepia ink and watercolour with notes on paper, 23.5 x 32 cm. Gennadeion Collection no. 113, Athens.

Gouvia

Nothing can be lovelier than those olive woods, when once the odious 3 miles of high road, the bane of Corfu, are accomplished. The olives in the northern centre of the island are not so fine, but younger, and if you go up to any of the hills you see all the landscape through the foliage just as if you looked through a thin veil. It is this effect I mean to try to get in one of my larger pictures. Then, as I sat drawing, the whole place is quite still, except that a hoopoe or a turtledove or an old raven, or a very large lizard, bright green and in a dreadful fuss, breaks the silence.

Kombitsi Monastery

Over the hill by Viros - the only time this winter I have seen those beautiful orange gardens I so constantly visited last year.

Kanoni

Then I walked on till I came to the Kanoni cliffs, where you see the little island called Ulysses' ship - and very charming it is: I made two drawings there today. There are two islands - I don't know which is the ship. You see hills of Benitses above them and I hardly fancy a prettier picture than the two make together. The nearer is a mere church and walls - the further a larger rock island . . . I slowly began to scramble all along the shadowed shore. Queer it is and no one knows why, that the sea recedes here for a week or so, *sans* rhyme or reason, and at other times you can't get around those rocks at all.

Myrtiotissa Monastery

In a little sheltered harbour - not uniike Amalfi - under great rocks, lies the little convent of

Myrtiotissa - so called from the myrtle covered cliffs all around. After my great Athos monasteries, this is a wee little one, with three monks only; however, it is clean and decent, and they gave us a cup of coffee each, which was not unwelcome.

Potamos

Then turn up towards Potamos, and thru' light-trunked olives, all filmy, the pool below, and the far snow range beyond seen through all the leafy dells and airy treetops. Then Potamos, with its clean and straw-hatted gray-trousered men, and its velvet-pelissed yellow-hooded respectable lovely women. And so very, very cold.

The South

Ano Pavliana

To Ano Pavliana . . . a difficult track, and one so slushy and steep I could hardly manage. However at the top is the village and Mr Charlton's house, a charming place of neatness of roses and gardens . . . The view over Lefkimi to Paxos is beautiful.

Aghios Nikolas

There is everywhere a flood of gold and green and blue . . . Just now the lilac range of Albanian mountains with the view pale but defined clouds above, the blue sky and the far deeper blue sea, the long almost blue plains of distant olives, and the still dark berryful cypresses close by - all bring back old memories. (What excessive contrast there is between the blooblooness of the sea and lilac hills, and the rich raw Sienna green of those cypresses!) . . . This Analipsis view is the most pleasing hereabouts, and were there welldrawn figures, it would be beautiful at sunset especially, when the mountains, by means of many detail-shadows, loose much of their wall-like form.

Aghios Procopios

. . . an idea of this beautiful place: the quiet warmth, and semi-shade are delightful . . . In these Prokopian holy glades are but three manifold colours: the warm pale green of the floor, with long shades, the gray uniform freckle-shimmer of the roof, with dark brown gray of the supporting pillartrunx. At 1 or 1.30, into the monastery and drew to 3 - awfully tortured by fleas, and obliged to stand in the sun all that time.

Gardiki (Paleokastro)

A castle like . . . any 12th Century gray-ivied walls, with immense olives about it. I drew on the hill till 12.30 - the long plain and the sea foamy, a beautiful scene, but the vast olives are for studies not sketches.

Hlomos

Hlomos itself is ugly, but the views are wonderful. The wind however was so that nothing could be done out of doors . . . Swallows twitter all around. (Little girl near Argirades tying up great red poppies in a wreath - 1st May . . . is the Mayday festivity a Greek one!) Of course, the very best view of Hlomos is just beyond the village.

Stavros

A pleasant shadeful walk . . . the olives *are* wonderful, the interminable perspective of the silver light-catching trunks contrasting with the deep shades on the green and fern below. Soon at Stavros - where a perlite [villager] showed us to the *topos* [place] where [all the English] were wont to go: and no lovelier view can be seen, so much so that I rank it first of all the distant Corfu views, as regards the seeing all and everything.

There was an Old Man of Corfu,
who never knew what he should do;
So he rushed up and down
till the sun made him brown,
That bewildered Old Man of Corfu.

Opposite page.
Edward Lear (1812-1888),
Inscribed and dated :
Viros 4 Feby 1863,
pencil, sepia ink, watercolour,
with notes on paper,
37.5 x 54.5 cm.
Gennadeion Collection, Athens.

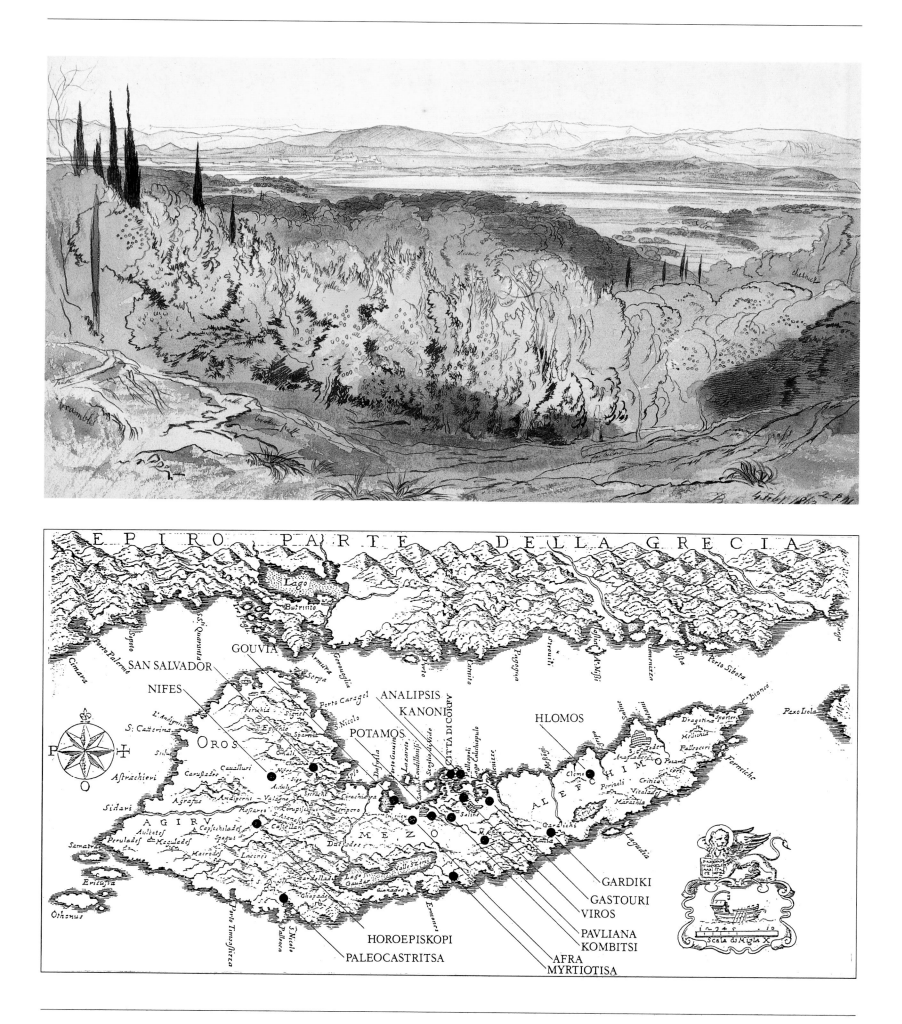

EPIRO PARTE DELLA GRECIA

GOUVIA

SAN SALVADOR

NIFES

ANALIPSIS
KANONI

POTAMOS

HLOMOS

GARDIKI
GASTOURI
VIROS

PAVLIANA
KOMBITSI

HOROEPISKOPI

PALEOCASTRITSA

AFRA
MYRTIOTISA

11 Music

Helena Matheopoulos

During the Dark Ages of Greece - the four centuries after the fall of Constantinople in 1453 - while the Greek mainland languished under Ottoman rule, Corfu and the other Ionian Islands enjoyed a Golden Age in almost every sense of the term, and especially as far as music and opera were concerned. As the capital city of a prized Venetian colony, Corfu was in a unique position to share the rich and varied Venetian musical and theatrical heritage for three and a half centuries (up to 1797), actively encouraged by the authorities, who stipulated that, among other things (such as the upkeep and disposition of his fleet), the Venetian naval commander was also responsible for arranging an annual visit by a *commedia dell'arte* company. The result was that Corfu and, to a lesser extent Zakinthos and the other Ionian Islands, became opera and theatre mad.

In the nineteenth century, as a British Protectorate, Corfu went even further; it developed a musical heritage of its own (which still constitutes the nucleus of modern Greek musical history) and produced native operatic composers whose works were performed and acclaimed not only locally but also in some of the greatest theatres of Italy and Germany.

From 1720, Corfu was also the proud possessor of the first theatre in Greece, an institution which came to be considered as one of the most important in the Eastern Mediterranean. The charming *Teatro San Giacomo*, now the Town Hall, named after the nearby Roman Catholic cathedral and completed in 1691, was originally a *loggia*, or club, for the nobility. These *loggias*, of which in the eighteenth century there were four, were frequented not only by the nobles inscribed

The Teatro di San Giacomo, shown here in an old print.

Opposite page.
Charalambos Pachis (1844-1891),
Celebrating the First of May,
oil on canvas, National Gallery,
Athens.

in the *Libro d'Oro* but also by select members of the cultivated upper bourgeoisie, and were the frequent venues of theatrical and musical performances. Before the conversion of the *Teatro San Giacomo* into a full-scale theatre, there was also a lively musical life taking place in town and village squares, with performances of straight or musical comedies - known as *Momaries* or *Bobaries*. But it was the conversion of the San Giacomo into a theatre and opera house (consisting of a stalls area of twelve rows, a gallery with ample space for standing room, and three tiers of boxes complete with *jalousies* and decorated individually, which could be hired for a whole season) that turned opera into a local cult and the Corfiot public into passionate, demanding and vociferous opera-lovers - worthy rivals of the most fanatical of Italian publics. So much so that the certificate *"Applaudito in Corfu"*, granted by the theatre's Governing Committee to artists who had won an ovation, came to be considered an almost instant passport to the great Italian and Western European theatres.

We know that the first opera to be performed at the San Giacomo (where straight plays were also staged), in 1733, was introduced by the Italian impresario Carlo Grassi; but we don't know its title or its composer. The destruction, by a German bomb on the night of 13-14 September 1943, of the priceless musical archive housed in the *Demotikon Theatron* resulted in severe gaps in our knowledge of the details of the theatre's programming. In fact, according to the *New Grove Dictionary of Opera* in which the sections on Greek music in general and Corfu in particular were compiled by the distinguished musicologist, critic and author George Leotsakos (to whom I am indebted for much of the information in this chapter), the only opera clearly identified as having been produced at the San Giacomo during the eighteenth century is Ferdinando Robuschi's *Castrini, Padre e Figlio*.

Fortunately we are infinitely better informed about the nineteenth century, a time when successive British High Commissioners were as actively enthusiastic about musical and operatic life as their Venetian predecessors. We know that the season ran from autumn to Christmas and from Boxing Day, through Carnival, to Lent.

A closer look at the former theatre of San Giacomo, now the Town Hall.

Opposite page. Decorative detail from the imposing façade of the present Town Hall.

A humble music lover of the nineteenth century. Watercolour from a private collection.

The Paganini of Corfu, a celebrated fiddler at the Opera. Watercolour, Private collection.

The theatre was governed by a committee of prominent music-loving citizens appointed by the Municipal Council. The Governing Committee wielded total artistic control: it arranged for annual visits by Italian companies and chose the works to be performed. If the public was not satisfied with the works at hand or with the performance standards, they jeered the Committee (no less savagely than today's Italian public jeer singers who sing less than perfectly), shouting *"a basso la Commissione"* (down with the Committee), which then had to resign. Needless to say, this became the main topic of conversation in the city, in the same way that the goings-on at the Opera House are the main conversation point for today's Viennese.

Most of the time, though, the public was more than satisfied. And with good reason. A glance through the list of operas performed at the San Giacomo in the nineteenth century proves that the Corfiot public was offered the cream of all new Italian operas within a season of their world premières in Italy. The list, preserved in the archives of Corfu's invaluable Reading Society (*Anagnostiki Etairia*), shows that the most popular composers were Rossini, Donizetti and Verdi. A typical sample of the repertoire put before the Corfiot public is, for instance, Rossini's *Semiramide* and *Tancredi* in 1826 and 1831 respectively, Bellini's *La Sonnambula* and *Norma* in 1834, Verdi's *Rigoletto* for three consecutive seasons from 1852 to 1855, Donizetti's *Lucrezia Borgia* in 1854, Meyerbeer's *Robert le Diable* in Italian in 1853, and Verdi's *I due Foscari* in 1859, with occasional rarities such as Xaverio Mercadante's *Elisa e Claudio* in 1801, interspersed with some Goldini comedies and plays such as Voltaire's tragedy *Mahomet* in 1821 and Racine's *Andromache* in Greek, performed by students of the Ionian Academy, in 1825. So it is clear that Corfu's cultural life was of a standard comparable to that of Europe's most sophisticated cities.

But the most significant and far-reaching development in the city's and, after 1864, the country's, musical life was the emergence, during the course of the nineteenth century, of several prominent native composers, usually educated in the world-famous Naples Conservatoire, who composed operas that were performed successfully not only in Corfu and Athens but also in Italy and Central Europe. The first opera by a Corfiot composer to be

performed at the San Giacomo was Nicholas Chalikiopoulos-Mantzaros' *Don Crepuscolo* in 1815, with a libretto in Italian. Four years later, Stefanos Poyanos produced a first attempt at a Greek opera, in fact a spectacle consisting of ballet with songs, *I para Faiaxin afixis tou Odysseos*, with words based on chapters 7 and 8 of *The Odyssey*, at the suggestion of the British High Commissioner, Sir Frederick Adam.

The list in the archives of the Reading Society shows that in the period from 1823 to 1889, seven operas by Greek composers, all with Italian libretti, were performed at the Teatro San Giacomo: Pavlos Carrer's *Isabella d'Aspeno* (1853) and *Rediviva* (1856); Spiros Xyndas' *Anna Winter* in 1855, based on *The Three Musketeers*, with Milady becoming the central character (an opera so enthusiastically received by the public that after the performance they unsaddled the horses from the composer's carriage and carried him home); Padovanis's *Dirce* (1857); Eduardo Lambelet's *Olema la schiava* (1857) and *Il castello maledetto* (1862); and Spiro Samaras' much-acclaimed *Flora Mirabilis*, which was also performed at La Scala. The first Greek opera

with a Greek libretto was Spiros Xyndas's *0 ypopsifios Vouleftis* (The Parliamentary Candidate), premièred at the *Teatro San Giacomo* in 1867, with an all-Corfiot cast. Stylistically, all the operas by the composers mentioned above were rooted in Italian *bel canto*, while the later operas of Spiros Samaras embraced *verismo* (literally realism, the style prevalent in the latter part of the nineteenth century).

Up to 1817 straight plays were also performed in Italian, but that year saw the staging of Iakovakis Rizos-Neroulos' five-act tragedy *Polyxeni*, published in Vienna three years earlier, and the occasion was considered historic enough for the British High Commissioner to be present. This was soon followed by a series of Greek tragedies performed in Greek by students of the Ionian Academy under the guidance of Lord Guilford, a great Philhellene. Patriotic feeling was running high at the time, because of the struggle for independence on the mainland, and composers and dramatists alike - not only Greeks but resident Italians as well - began to draw their inspiration from the heroes of modern Greece instead of antiquity. Giovanni Battista Ferrari

*Emblem on show at
the headquarters of the
Corfu town choir.*

*The emblem of Corfu's Musical
Society for "Kantades" (ballads).*

wrote a five-act opera based on the siege of Souli, *Gli ultimi giorni di Suli,* which was premièred in 1842 at the Teatro La Fenice in Venice, and performed in Cephalonia in 1859-60 and at the Teatro San Giacomo in Corfu in 1867, while Rafael Parisini wrote *Arkadion,* based on the Cretan uprising of 1866. The Corfiot Pavlos Carrer also produced operas based on heroes of the Greek War of Independence: *Markos Botsaris* and *I Kyra Frossini.* Greek plays and operas drew a strong response from the Corfiot audience who, despite their Italianate culture and customs, nevertheless felt themselves one hundred per cent Greek.

During the nineteenth century, the Teatro Giacomo also became the venue for the first symphony concerts on Greek soil, performed by the orchestras set up by the first musical association in Greece: the Saint Spyridon Philharmonic Society, founded in 1840 with the express aim of providing a brass band for the annual procession of Saint Spyridon, the island's patron saint. Up to then, the British authorities had always assigned a military detachment and brass band to attend the celebrations, but in 1837 the government in London issued an order

forbidding British military bands to take part in religious ceremonies of any kind. This caused great offence to the islanders, who interpreted it as an insult to their religious traditions, hitherto respected by all Corfu's foreign rulers. On 11 August 1837, when the procession reached the balcony where the High Commissioner was standing, a group of angry young men threw their candles in the air in protest.

Shortly after this bandless procession, it was decided that something must be done to remedy the situation. Nine young men came together to form a society which would provide a band for the procession of the saint. It therefore decided to call itself the Saint Spyridon Philharmonic. Its premises were inaugurated in September 1840 and the band it assembled and trained made its first appearance the following year, at the Saint Spyridon procession of 11 November 1841. Two of the first honorary members of the Saint Spyridon Philharmonic were Admiral Clarence Page, an ardent Philhellene, and the composer Gioacchino Rossini. These were joined in 1859 by the last British High Commissioner, Sir Henry Storks, and in 1874 by the French composer Charles Gounod.

The Saint Spyridon Philharmonic came to be known as the 'old' Philharmonic, to distinguish it from the 'new' Philharmonic Society, founded in 1890 and called the Mantzaros Philharmonic, in honour of the composer of the Greek National Anthem who died in 1872. Mantzaros used to give free tuition at the old Philharmonic and was named its President for life. It was thanks to the music school he had founded on the island after his return from Naples that there was a group of well trained musicians at hand for the Saint Spyridon Philharmonic to draw from for its brass band. Both Philharmonics provided and continue to provide, well trained orchestral musicians for ensembles such as the Athens State Orchestra and the orchestra of the National Lyric Stage, as well as players for the island's eleven brass bands: four in Corfu city - where they are a familiar sight at the Victorian Bandstand on the upper Esplanade opposite the Cavalieri Hotel - and seven in various villages, the oldest of which is the Gastouri band, founded in 1898.*

The importance of musical education for the continuation of any nation's musical life and tradition was tirelessly stressed by the most important figure in the island's musical life

during the nineteenth century, Nicholas Chalikiopoulos Mantzaros (1795-1872), universally known and beloved as the composer of the Greek National Anthem, to the poem 'A Hymn to Freedom' by his close friend, the poet Dionysios Solomos. King George I of the Hellenes, who heard it performed by the Saint Spyridon Philharmonic Society band during his visit to Corfu in 1864, decreed that it should henceforth become the nation's official anthem.

Mantzaros had returned to his native Corfu to devote himself body and soul to teaching the younger generation, despite an invitation by his teacher, the distinguished composer Nicola Zingarelli, to succeed him as the Director of the prestigious Naples Conservatoire. He was an idealist who passionately believed in the spiritual role of music as a force in a civilised society, and personally financed and oversaw the musical education of countless poor students,

* *One of the lasting memories of visitors to Corfu town is of the Philharmonic bands rehearsing, which they do in upper rooms with the windows open, so that the rich, brassy sounds float out and envelop the neighbouring streets and squares.*

*Pages 190 & 191.
Brass-helmeted bandsmen
marching through Corfu town.*

aided by his pupils Anthony Liveralis and Spyros Xyndas. He is commemorated by a plaque outside his house at 26 St Basil Street.

Although one can hardly overestimate his influence on Corfu's musical life, as a composer pure and simple Mantzaros was not prolific. Apart form the opera *Don Crepusculo* mentioned above, he composed four symphonies and various other pieces, mostly cantatas, both religious and secular. In purely musical terms, the most distinguished Corfiot composer was undoubtedly Spiros Samaras (1861-1917), who studied in Athens, France and Italy and became internationally famous. Two of his operas, *Flora Mirabilis* and *Rhea*, were performed at La Scala and Munich and published by the distinguished Milanese House of Sonzogno (whose archives perished in a war-time air raid). His equally popular *La martire*, which contains truly beautiful arias, has just been recorded. Samaras is also famous as the composer of the Olympic Hymn, to verses by the poet Kostis Palamas, which was first heard at the first modern Olympics, in 1896, at the Athens Stadium. In 1958 the Olympic Committee in Tokyo proclaimed it the official Olympic Hymn.

Amusingly enough, Samaras is also famous, indirectly, for his single failure: the opera *Lionella*, premièred at La Scala on 14 April 1891 but now lost. Although, in the composer's own admission, it was not a success, it nevertheless contained some exquisite passages, including a *romanza* which surfaced a year later as Canio's heartbraking aria, *Ridi Pagliaccio*, in Leoncavallo's opera *I Pagliacci*, reportedly with Samaras' blessing. Another lost work by Samaras is *La furia domata*, based on Shakespeare's *The Taming of the Shrew* and premièred at Milan's Teatro Lirico Internazionale on 19 November 1895.

Samaras' two lost operas are, tragically, a mere drop in the ocean of lost Greek operas, of which there are about forty-five, i.e. a third of all 135 known Greek operas (according to recent research by George Leotsakos). Some manuscripts may still be buried (and in some cases are *known* to be buried) in dusty chests of drawers in Corfu's country estates, often in the hands of descendants too indifferent even to bother to look for them. But most manuscripts, both scores and libretti, were destroyed in the German raid which razed the *Demotikon Theatron*

A festive scene at the Strada Reale in Corfu town in 1840.

Opposite page.
Built during the British rule of the island, this ornate Victorian bandstand in the centre of the esplanade would be at home in Kensington Gardens.

(the Municipal Theatre) to the ground, along with the Ionian Academy, with its priceless archives spanning the entire musical history of the island. What information we do possess is largely thanks to the lists of libretti and other sources preserved at the Reading Society.

The *Demotikon Theatron* had been erected to replace the Teatro San Giacomo, which became the city Town Hall. It was inaugurated on 7 December 1902 with the first performance in Greece of Wagner's *Lohengrin* and was considered one of the most beautiful in Europe - 39 metres high and magnificent.

Its stage was huge and the acoustics perfect. In pictures its façade looks highly reminiscent of the Vienna State Opera. After the foundation of Dionysios Lavrangas' company Ellinikon Melodrama (Greek melodrama, i.e. Greek Opera Company), visits by Italian companies alternated with visits by this company, performing both operas and operettas, Viennese and Greek. After the bombardment of Corfu town and the brief occupation of the island by Italian Fascists in 1923, visits by Italian companies were suspended.

Yet even the destruction of its gem of a theatre could not stem the flow of the island's musical life. Its Philharmonic Societies - to which was added a third, called after Capodistrias - its excellent Conservatoire, founded in 1894, with classes for piano, violin, mandolin and children's choir, plus its many choirs and bands are as vigorous as ever. In admitting women to its bands, Corfu was again a pioneer in Greece.

The island's music continues to delight visitors, both foreign and Greek - an indication perhaps, of what the musical life of the whole nation could have been had Constantinople not fallen to the Ottomans in 1453.

12 The Flowers of Corfu

Ann Nash

At any time of the year, a first impression of Corfu is certainly a lush, green one, especially compared to the barren Aegean islands. This is due to the hundreds of evergreen olives, cypresses, bushes and shrubs. Only in the summer is there almost no grass to be seen. The island is situated in a sheltered position surrounded by a warm sea, and with a heavy rainfall. The winters are warmer than on the mainland, but with occasional frost and even a little snow on the highest peak of Mount Pantocrator (906 metres; 2972 feet). However, the winter climate seems to be changing. In 1991 it snowed three times, the snow once settling all over the island and not completely disappearing for a week; a rare occurrence. This was followed by two months of frost. So frost and ice are more prevalent now, and the rainfall less.

Over the years the island has changed considerably, mostly round the coast and the main roads. Roads have been widened, and there

has been, and still is, non-stop building everywhere. Many plant habitats have thus been lost. However, there are still plenty of good areas inland for flowers, especially in the more remote and unspoilt parts.

In January and February the first few anemones appear, and by April there is a mass everywhere, in lovely colours from purple, magenta, mauve, pink to almost white. The first orchid is an early one, the giant orchid (*barlia robertina*). It has a tall spike of greenish or green/pink flowers and can reach nearly 40 cm. in height. Although not very colourful, a colony of plants make a fine sight - I have seen one patch of fifty. Another early plant is the little iris (*iris unguicularis*). Gradually through March and April the flora are in full swing. The bee orchids (*ophrys*) begin to flower, so called as they are supposed to resemble insects. In fact, the bumblebee orchid (*ophrys bombyliflora*) does just that with its tiny brown and green flowers. One of the most striking is the

A floral study loosely based on the flowers of Corfu, by Mildred Flamburiari.

Orchis Quadripunctata: the wild four-spotted orchid.

Opposite page: Orlaya and vicia create a lovely springtime picture.

woodcock orchid (*ophrys scolopax s.s.p.cornuta*), with a beautifully marked lip of patterns in wine, green and white, with the lobes of the lip as two sharp pointed horns. The most common are the horseshoe, which has a horseshoe pattern on the lip, and lutea, a delicate little brown and yellow ophrys.

In early spring the Greek hellebore (*helleborus cyclophyllus*) flowers, an attractive plant in spite of its green flowers; but it is poisonous. Another not very colourful plant is the widow iris (*hermodactylus tuberosus*), with greenish-yellow flowers and the petals almost black. The squirting cucumber (*ecballium elaterium*) is an intriguing plant, found growing in stony waste places. With rough textured leaves and yellow flowers, the seed pod is like a tiny cucumber, and when ripe, bursts with quite a mini-explosion. A flower-tour client who used to visit Corfu nearly every year had never seen the seed pods, so I sent him one in a matchbox; needless to say it had burst on arrival.

Wild flowers usually abound in the British cemetery on Corfu.

Opposite page.
Gladioli make a brilliant splash of colour.

The sheer mass of spring flowers are too many to enumerate. It is a truly marvellous panorama of colour, a field of pink geranium and white daisies, another area all pink from another plant of the daisy family - crepis; large brilliant blue patches of lupins; hillsides covered with yellow broom (*spartium junceum*), and the spiny broom (*calicotome villosa*); fields of asphodel, and sheets of star of Bethlehem; more hills ablaze with pink and white cistus, and wild white roses scrambling everywhere, a lovely sight growing up the odd cypress tree.

What better place to start a flower tour of the island than the British Cemetery in Corfu town? It does not have a typical cemetery feel to it. It is like a sheltered, private garden, an oasis in an urban setting. There are cultivated flowers, many wild orchids and magnificent trees. It is looked after by George Psailas, as it was by his father before him, and the family have lived in the house since 1924. George has been in charge for forty years, and in 1977 was awarded a certificate of honour by the Commonwealth War Graves Commission. He is knowledgeable about the orchids, and has learnt the names, and has also produced an interesting little booklet about the cemetery. Many botanists and other visitors make a visit a "must", especially for the orchids, which are so thick on the ground it is difficult not to tread on them. The grass is never cut until the orchids are over and have seeded.

Amongst the orchids are a few monkey orchids (*ophrys simia*), which are not too plentiful at coastal level. They are usually marked with sticks, so that visitors will not miss them. Once on a visit I noticed an enchanting little monkey (an animal, not the orchid) sitting on the cemetery wall. George asked me if I had seen it and I wanted to know whom it belonged to and where it had come from. For several minutes we were talking at cross-purposes, he about the *orchid*, I about the *animal*. It transpired that there was a Veterinary Clinic next door, and probably the monkey had got loose and scrambled on to the wall.

Away from the town, the long sandy beaches of the west and north coasts provide a good example of marine flora, as do the areas around Lake Korission in the south, the salt-pans at Alikes, and in the north the lagoon of Andinioti, to the west of Kassiopi. Perhaps this site is the most interesting, as so far the only development

is along the narrow road down to the lagoon and beach, with just a small tavern and a church there. From the church, a sandy track behind the beach leads to a bridge over the inlet from the sea to the lagoon. Beyond the bridge is a large wild area full of plants; several different orchids include fine specimens of purple loose-flowered orchids, which like a damp habitat amongst the reeds and sea lavender bordering the lake. Tongue orchids are happy here too, and some large specimens are to be seen. They are so named because of the long, down-pointing lip. They are not always easy to identify as they vary enormously and often cross with another of a different species.

At the back of the beach are low clumps of dyer's alkanet (*alkanna tinctoria*) with brilliant blue flowers. A red dye was once extracted from the root. Lower down the beach, stocks flower, and a very spiny cushion belonging to the cow parsley family (*umbelliferae*); it has white flowers but only the Greek/Latin name *echinophora spinosa* is used. The most beautiful plant here is the sea daffodil, or sand lily (*pancratium maritimum*). From clumps of large, broad leaves arise the lovely white flowers from July onwards. (They are also to be found on some other beaches such as those of Agios Gordis, Glifada and Agios Stefanos on the west coast.)

A walk in the opposite direction past the taverna reveals another untouched wild area both sides of the road. Flowers abound, orchids including the pink butterfly, several species of tongue orchids and bee orchids. Patches of blue will be lupins, and then there is wild garlic, the pink and rose-coloured forms, geranium, grape hyacinth, flax, crepis, mullein, sage and many species of the pea family. On the far beach is the sea spurge, and sea holly, the rocky outcrop behind the small house is a mass of stock. Bird-watchers will enjoy this area and should look out for heron, egret, gull and waders.

Continuing south-eastwards along the coast to Kassiopi, with a magnificent view of Albania, shrubs of wild sumach adorn the roadside. Higher above the banks blue lupins make a fine show and also a very pretty blue sage. In May and June campanulas flower, another gorgeous blue.

Kassiopi is almost a town now, but the harbour waterfront is still attractive, surrounded by cafes, tavernas, and local boats. A rewarding walk is up a path to the left of the harbour. It used to be a marvellous place for flowers, but unfortunately villas have been built, and the ground scrubbed up in places, so there is not the profusion of plants now. On your left is a pretty tree, the

Indian bead tree (*melia azaderach*). It is a native of China and there are quite a lot of them over the island. In May and June they bear blue flowers and pinnate leaves, followed by round yellow fruit that remains on the tree all winter, nearly into spring. The fruit was once used for rosary beads, but this was discontinued when it was discovered that the seeds were poisonous.

The path leads on to a headland, and the hill where there are the remains of a Venetian fortress. Here you will still find some good Tongue orchids, including one which only grows in Corfu, Zakinthos and Cephalonia. It is *Serapia neglecta s.s.p ionica*. A rather unusual mullein grows here; the flowers are a violet shade, sometimes bronze, not yellow as the other species.

Beyond Kassiopi, going south, is the turning down to Agios Stefanos (not to be confused with the place of the same name on the west coast). This is tree heather country, tall shrubs growing above the road and covering the hills running to the coast to the left of the watch-tower.

Along the Nissaki-Barbati road and on the hillsides above, is a tall yellow plant which is woad (*isatis tinctoria*). The blue dye was extracted from the dying leaves. From now on the east coast is too developed until the southernmost tip of the island.

The road to Lakones, an attractive village above Paleokastritsa, provides good plants and fine views. There is a large patch of tree euphorbia on the way up, growing out of a high cliff. When flowering it is a brilliant green and yellow. It seems to grow only in this area and in some spots down the coast from Paleokastritsa.

Beyond the village is the popular cafe stop of Bella Vista, with a fine view to Paleokastritsa below and down the rugged west coast with its high cliffs and small bays. Here along the rocky banks are yellow rock rose, germander, prasium - a small shrub with white flowers - and an attractive woundwort.

Continuing on the road to Krini, Angelocastro comes into view, the remains of the castle atop a high rocky hill, with a tiny church at the summit. Not a great deal survives except the walls. Approaching the castle from the village,

the rough stony ground is a blaze of white cistus. It is a small, narrow-leaved variety with small flowers. More rock roses abound, iris and orchids on the terraces above.

But of all the botanical areas of Corfu, Pantokrator is richest in plants; over one hundred different species have been recorded. Several of these only grow at that height: candytuft, saxifrage, eastern bugle, asphodel, and a most lovely pale blue veronica.

In February and March the ground is carpeted with blue anemones (*anemone blanda*) and tiny scillas (*scilla bifolia*). Later in mid-May several areas are a true rock-garden, with honesty, anemone, saxifraga, anchusa, euphorbia, dead nettle, asphodeline, grape hyacinths, bugle, alyssum and veronica. The prostrate euphorbia (*euphorbia myrsinites*) only grows up here, as does the attractive dead nettle (*lamium garganicum*), with pink flowers. The botanical prize of Pantocrator must go to the fritillaries, *fritillaria graeca* and *fritillaria messanensis*, slender plants about 10-15 cm. tall, with narrow leaves. The flowers are hanging bells, browny green and faintly chequered and striped on the outside. An interesting plant is the burning bush (*dictamnus albus*), which is very aromatic and contains oil which is supposed to burn if ignited. It flowers in June, and due to fire danger it is not recommended to put a match to it.

Low-growing clumps of soapwort (*saponaria calabrica*) decorate the roadside banks from above Strinilas onwards, a marvellous pink against the white-ish rocks. Many orchids will be seen, among them the man orchid (*aceras anthropophorum*), Three-toothed orchid (*orchis tridentata*), yellow Provence (*orchis provincialis*) with spotted leaves, and another yellow orchid - pauciflora, and the magenta four-spotted orchid (*orchis quadripunctata*); more often than not the latter has three or five spots on the lip and not four. Bee orchids are also here, the horseshoe, lutea and sawfly (*ophrys tenthredinifera*). Monkey orchids can be found but are not very common.

The monastery at the summit of Pantocrator, from which there are breath-taking views, is often open in the morning, but there are no monks there now; it is looked after by a Papas from a village lower down. Birds to look for are rock thrush, buzzard, falcon and peregrine.

Walking once on the north side of the mountain, I missed the correct way down to Old Perithia, the half-deserted village below the summit. Rather than turn back I continued on down an extremely steep and rough hillside. What a reward! The entire hillside was covered with fritillaries and yellow orchids. Never have I seen such a display. On the same day I made another discovery, one plant of leopards' bane (*doronicum*). I have never found it on the island before, as it is really a plant from the mainland.

Opposite page:
Antirrhinum, with its orange and
yellow flowers, looks well against
the summer sky.

Campanula ramosissima lends a dramatic burst of mauve to the green background.

Opposite page.
Pink mallow and rosa penelope decorate this corner of a garden.

A day excursion to Old Perithia is very rewarding both for the flowers and for the old village. The site of the original village lay where New Perithia is now, down at the coastal level. After a time the people feared attacks from pirates and built their village higher up, completely hidden from the coast. On the way up to Loutses the rocky hills are colourful with yellow asphodeline and turpentine trees (*pistacia terebinthus*). The latter have small clusters of red flowers followed by red fruit, and the crushed leaves produce a turpentine smell. In late May tall delphiniums grace the olive-groves beside the road. As you climb higher there is a sea of olives almost to the coast, part of the Andinioti lagoon comes into view, and to the west the beaches of Akharavi and Roda. In spring there will be cherry blossom and flowering ash.

The tarmac road continues a little way out of the village of Loutses, thereafter becoming somewhat rough. All the time cars bump up and down in the season. It is only one hour's walk to Old Perithia, but is well worth the effort for the natural rock garden on the way. Apparently growing out of the stony road is a delicate blue iris (*gynandriris sisyrinchium*). It is a very reliable clock, only opening after lunch. Campanulas, rock roses, grape hyacinths, yellow Provence orchids and the four-spotted orchid grow amongst the rocks. High above the banks will be many yellow asphodeline, also the more common pink and white one. In the deep valley below are many oak-trees, and there are a few on one of the corners of the road. Here if you are lucky, you may see one of the most beautiful birds, the golden oriole; they particularly like oak-trees.

Old Perithia is a large village, built on two hills, and a wander around is full of interest. The old stone buildings have much charm and character, although many are in a ruinous state. One family lives there permanently, but the other people have all moved lower down to other villages. Some of them return in the summer with their sheep and goats. Now there is an excellent cafe/taverna open from late April till the end of September. There are fine trees in the village including cherry, walnut, almond, oak and a nettle tree. Roses scramble everywhere amongst the brambles and ground elder entangles the ruins.

The area inland behind Gouvia and Kontokali, between the Paleokastritsa road and the Ropa valley, is a favourite place for walkers and flower-lovers. Still unspoilt and with many tracks and paths, flowers abound. There are two small lakes and several ponds, where there are terrapins and pond tortoises and, of course, hundreds of frogs. It is a damp area and so the right habitat for tongue orchids and the loose-flowered orchid. I once counted hundreds of the latter in one small area. Other orchids are plentiful too. Also to be found here and in many other places is a plant belonging to the cow parsley family (*umbelliferae*) called orlaya. A tall plant with large umbels of beautiful white flowers, the outer flowers have longer petals, and the whole is rather like a delicate piece of embroidery or crochet. In early spring the fields near the lakes are dotted with little clumps of wild narcissus (*narcissus tazetta*). In this area live pine martens, but they are not often to be seen. Foxes exist too, but it is doubtful if there are many left now, as a devastating fire right through this area probably killed many animals.

The long summer is hot and dry, and therefore few flowers are to be seen. Some quite colourful thistles bloom, the most striking being *eryngium amethystinum*, the same family as the sea holly. The electric blue colour is quite dazzling. In August flowers a member of the lily family, the sea squill (*urginea maritima*): from large bulbs arise thick stems up to 12 metres tall, with spikes of small white flowers. Another plant flowering in the summer is *inula viscosa*, a leafy, shrubby

In purest white, orlaya grandiflora.

Opposite page: Salvia guarantitica adds its gentle perfume to the garden.

206

A wonderful bush of chrysanthemum frutescens as seen in Lady Holmes's beautiful garden.

Opposite page: Chrysanthemum coronarium, with its bright yellow flowers is to be found all over Corfu.

plant with yellow-daisy-like flowers, and very aromatic sticky leaves. It can be seen growing at the edges of the road in many places.

Autumn is a welcome respite after the summer's heat, like a second spring when, after the first rains, green grass appears once again. Not long after, the cyclamen, autumn crocus, and clumps of golden sternbergia begin to bloom. There is even an autumn orchid, autumn lady's tresses (*spiranthes spiralis*), the tiny white flowers in a spiral up the stem. The strawberry tree flowers and fruits. In the past, the peasants made a drink from the strawberry-like fruit.

Fields and olive groves will be carpeted with mauve autumn crocus, and another little creamy white crocus with red stigmas - *crocus boryi*. Corfu's wild snowdrop (*galanthus corcyrensis*) blooms in November and December, making white sheets in damp and shady places.

Many different indigenous trees are to be seen apart from the olive and cypress. There are pine, oak, chestnut, walnut, almond, plane, elm, tamarisk, flowering ash, bay, poplar and carob to mention a few. The latter have long seed pods hanging from the branches, and the seeds were once used for the carat weight of gold.

In the spring the Judas-trees make a fine splash of colour throughout the island. They are so called because Judas Iscariot is reputed to have hanged himself from one. The wild pear is now a mass of white blossom, followed by tiny, very hard fruit. Gradually more blossom comes forth from almond, pear, peach, apple and quince.

Amongst the introduced trees are jacaranda, false acacia, eucalyptus, castor-oil tree, acacia, osage orange, and the Indian bead tree. The osage orange (*maclura pomifera*) comes from South America, and is named in honour of William Maclure, a geologist. It was introduced into England in 1818, so possibly some early traveller brought seeds or cuttings to Corfu. A large spiny tree, it is used in America for hedges. The fruit is very unusual, like a large round lemon with a wrinkled skin. Inside it resembles a pickled brain, as some botanists refer to it. It is not edible. There is one tree at Kassiopi near the harbour and a couple along the Garitsa waterfront. Sweet and horse chestnuts are on the island, the latter very striking when in flower: they grow wild on the mainland but have probably been planted in the town for ornament.

Much of Corfu is covered with maquis; that is where there are few trees but many shrubs, including Kermes oak, spiny broom, Jerusalem sage, lentisc, myrtle, thyme, butcher's broom, cistus and buckthorn. The Kermes oak has small, spiny leaves, not unlike holly. Its Latin name, *quercus coccifera*, refers to the red galls to be found on it, which are scale insects - *coccus illicis*; these produce a red dye for cochineal.

In damp areas grows the chaste tree or monk's pepper, more of a large shrub, so called because the seeds were supposed to suppress sexual feelings. Christ's thorn is one of the most spiny shrubs, but attractive with its bright green leaves and small yellow flowers. It is believed that Christ's crown of thorns may have been made from this shrub.

Apart from the tree heather in spring, there is autumn-flowering heather (*erica verticillara*) in shades of purple, mauve and pinky white.

Occasionally a strange plant can be found growing on cistus roots, a parasite. It looks like a tomato cut in half and stuffed with scrambled egg.

This old stone staircase is enhanced by decorative trailing geraniums.

The flowers are yellow and enclosed in bright red scales. Another parasite, to be found on the pea and sage families, is broomrape, in several species that from a distance almost resemble an orchid. Some are quite attractive, especially those with blue flowers, and the clove-scented broomrape can grow to 30 cm. or more. One of the orchids, *limodorum*, has no green leaves and some authorities say it might be parasitic on tree roots, but this is doubtful. However, it is a fine plant, 30-70 cm. tall with a thick purple stem and violet flowers. Then there is the gardener's bane, dodder. Try unwinding it from petunias!

Many parts of the island are still untouched and off the beaten track. Walks of several hours can be made through valleys without seeing a house, and perhaps the only people are a few peasants working in an olive-grove or on their vegetable plot. In the spring a few of the valleys have enchanting little streams running through them, with mini-waterfalls and rock pools.

Care should be taken over snakes. There are plenty around, but only one is dangerous, the Eastern sand viper which tends to lie in wait before finally moving away. May and June, when it is really warming up, bring the snakes out. Walking in long grass or amongst bushes, it is a good idea to carry a stick and bang it in front of you. Nearly always snakes sense or hear your approach and rustle away.

All the rustling in the grass and bushes is not necessarily a snake. The large Balkan lizard makes quite a noise; a fine sight, it is brilliant green with a yellow underside. Tortoises also make a noise in the undergrowth, especially when mating, as their shells bang together.

No need for a herb garden as the following grow wild: fennel, oregano, thyme, rosemary, sage mint, dill, borage and bay. Oregano (*rigani* in Greek), much used in Greek cooking, is gathered in early July and dried. Camomile is harvested and dried for tea, which is good for colds, constipation, skin disorders and supposedly hangovers. The three-lobed sage is also used as a tea.

There are at least four hundred different species of wild flowers in Corfu, which is why the island attracts many flower-lovers, professional and amateur. Needless to say, picking the flowers is not encouraged, digging them up still less so.

Opposite page:
An old ceramic pot is surrounded
by exotic looking flowering aloes.

Old buildings and rolling terrain combine to create a scene of peace and beauty.

13 With a Camera's Eye

*Time stands still in the green
and grey summer landscape.*

Well worn steps lead to the entrance of a country house.

Opposite page
A lovely old stone porch discovered in a nearly forgotten village.

*A study in old masonry and
new leaf.*

*Opposite page.
This gnarled old olive tree has
survived through the centuries.*

A fishing boat rides at anchor, at peace before the night's work commences.

Opposite page.
A dramatically different fishing craft.

*An old peasant sells his oranges
from hand-made wicker baskets.*

*Opposite page.
Top. A basket weaver plies
his trade.
Bottom. The finished article:
Baskets for sale!*

A monk awaits his leisurely cup of coffee at a cheerful wayside café.

Opposite page.
An old monk takes time off from
his meditations to pose for the
camera.

A group of 'Kaikia', fishing boats,
caught in the sun's golden rays.

A rickety jetty, used by fishermen, wends its way into the sea.

One of the many old bell towers dotted around the island.

Opposite page. Silhouetted against the sky, a handsome bell tower in rich Venetian pink.

Brilliantly-hued flowers add a
splash of colour to this village
street scene.

Opposite page.
Siesta time in an old country
village.

A crusty combination of old steps, wall and portico in a village in the north east of the island.

*Opposite page.
These colourful umbrellas have been strategically placed to keep the sun away from a wrought iron balcony in the town.*

A shopping precinct in the old town.

Opposite page.
The Reading Society's building in the foreground and town mansions behind.

A green and pleasant land.

'Where sheep may safely graze…'

This beautiful camellia grows well
in Corfu.

Opposite page.
A brilliant pink flowering bush
comes to life again every Spring.

A fine old doorway.

Ornate door of the church at Kinopiastes, the picturesque village where Edward Lear spent some time.

Village scene. Filling a pitcher at
the well.

Opposite page.
Sailors taking part in a procession
through the town.

242

An old stone archway leads us to a country dwelling.

Opposite page.
The stark architecture of the new fortress towers above the town.

This page and opposite.
Magnificent old buildings seen
from the sea.

Rear view taken from sea of the palace of St. Michael and St. George.

Greek flags enhance the faded elegance of a typical Corfiot façade.

The tiled rooftops of Corfu town with the sea beyond.

The unmistakable landmark of
St. Spyridon's church towering
above the rooftops.

Small boats bob up and down on a
blue summer sea with the old
fortress in the background.

Opposite page.
Approaching the Venetian villa at
Kombitsi through a haze of wild
flowers.

A typical Venetian chimney seen at the villa on the estate at Kombitsi.

Opposite page.
This Venetian fountain on the estate at Kombitsi, formerly owned by Andrew and Sonia Sinclair, is approached by a secluded cobbled path. One of Corfu's landmarks, it has provided the purest water for the past three hundred years.

Dark cypresses stand tall and emerge from a densely green landscape.

*This brightly lit naval aircraft
carrier at anchor off the coast of
Corfu lends a festive touch to the
sky at dawn.*

Cricketers enjoy a game on the Esplanade, or Spianada, under the protective shadow of the old fort in Corfu town.

14 Cricket

Lord Orr-Ewing OBE

During the forty-nine years of the British Protectorate, cricket was played regularly by members of the military garrison, visiting ships from the British Mediterranean fleet, and expatriates enjoying the hospitality of this beautiful island. According to John Forte, who did more than anyone to re-establish cricket after the Second World War, the earliest known date for a cricket match was 23 April 1823.

Matches are played on the Spianada, shared nowadays between cricket and carparking. Until recently, the field itself had the consistency of the gravel on the Horse Guards Parade in London.

Unfortunately, it is also home to many discarded bottle-tops and some broken glass. As the ball is hit towards the fielder, it jumps from pebble to pebble. The Corfiot teams excel in their fielding, and the island's cricketers are generally to be recognised by the scars on their kneecaps.

All matches played are limited to thirty-three overs. Play (the word in Corfu means cricket) officially begins at 2.30 pm but seldom starts until well after 3. Owing to the intense heat, there are welcome breaks for drinks, conveniently close to the cafés whose chairs and tables, under the arches of the neighbouring French-built Colonnade, mark the leg boundary.

Members of the British garrison playing cricket on November 29, 1860, on the same pitch still used today.

If the visiting team is batting second, the Corfiot cricketers have an understandable tendency to drag out the game until well after 8 pm, when, as the season advances, batsmen are dazzled in the fading evening by the lights of cars driving round the Spianada.

Further challenges are the long conferences indulged in by Corfiot teams and the conversations they carry on while the balls are being bowled.

During the thirty years I have been involved in Corfiot cricket, intense competition has taken place between the local clubs, whose number has varied between two and four. The two oldest are Gymnastikos and Byron, a sort of Greek variation on the theme of Gentlemen v. Players (though the poet, not notable as a cricketer, never set foot on the island). In an incident when feelings were running especially high, one of the clubs involved captured the key of the changing-room, where much of the kit was stored, and locked the other one out. The match had to be cancelled.

In 1971, I helped to found the Anglo-Corfiot Cricket Association (ACCA) and became its President. Its aim is to promote and sponsor cricket in the island. Then in 1976 came a major development: the Greek Ministry of Sport took over responsibility for cricket in Corfu. Their continuing financial support has contributed to the encouragement of cricket and the remarkable growth in foreign tours. In recent years, these have included visits to Malta and Cyprus, while Corfu, in the name of Greece, has participated in the last two European cups held in Guernsey and England.

Many English clubs now visit Corfu. They include the Lords Taverners, British Airways, the Cricketers' XI, and the Cricket Society, which has what could be called a special relationship with Corfiot cricket. It has toured the island many times, and in 1974 had the Laws of Cricket translated into Greek - although there is not much evidence that the Corfiots heed the fact. The Society also helps to bring young Corfiot cricketers to England for coaching and has provided cricket kit for them at home.

Memories of Anglo-Corfiot encounters include the episode in 1982 when a strong Cricket Society side, having beaten all the local teams, confronted an all-Corfu side in a final 'Test match'. In their thirty-three overs the Corfiots had made 176 for 7 wickets. Although both scorers had correctly recorded this, the scoreboard showed 177. By the last ball of the last over, the Cricket Society's score stood at 175 for 7. After several prolonged tactical conferences among the fielding side, and as darkness gathered, it was agreed between the two English batsmen that even if the one at the receiving end failed to make contact with the ball (which is what happened) he and his colleague at the other end should run for it. They did, a bye was awarded, and the match was over.

The all-Corfu XI, still believing that the scoreboard was right, rejoiced in victory. But when it was pointed out that the scores were level, pandemonium broke out. The fifteen-year-old Corfiot scorer, surrounded by his angry countrymen, courageously insisted his scorebook was accurate. The English wondered whether a diplomatic retreat was called for. But after fifteen minutes of hot dispute the Corfiots realised that they had never yet played in a tie, and this historic result was celebrated in a wonderful Anglo-Greek dinner at Paleokastritsa.

Another example of the unique atmosphere of these Spianada battles was a game in 1970 between two English visiting teams. The top-scoring batsman so impressed a Corfiot onlooker that he there and then offered his grand-daughter's hand in marriage to the surprised cricketer - an offer that was graciously declined.

During the late 1970s and early 1980s, two all-rounders from the Gymnastikos and Byron teams dominated Corfu cricket. Both were then married to English girls. Their styles reflected their clubs. Iannis Arvanitakis of Gymnastikos, tall and elegant, was the first Corfiot player to receive professional coaching in England. He bowled with a classical high action and batted very correctly with a straight bat. During later years, he worked in Athens but would return to Corfu for big games.

On one occasion, tired after his journey, he bowled seven overs of immaculate length and direction before retiring to a chair at the deep point boundary from where he directed his side.

The Esplanade seen from the Royal Palace, a drill ground for troops since Venetian times and cricket ground for close on 150 years.

Spiro Kantaros, of Byron, was a plumber, stocky with short curly hair. He bowled almost round-arm; his batting was and remains unpredictable. When his first daughter was born, he came to England for a year. One of the first games he played there was in the Isle of Wight. When his turn came to bat, the first ball he received was fast and of good length. Orthodox cricketers might have hoped to play it defensively. Spiro hit it with a cross bat straight back past the astonished bowler to the boundary.

(I am grateful to Michael de Navarro QC, former team secretary of the Cricket Society XI, and to Christopher Box-Grainger, also of the Cricket Society, for their input to this article.)

Here are a few examples, extracted from John Forte's book*, of Corfiot cricketing terminology:

Bails	*Rollinia* (from the Italian)
Batsman	*Batsman*
Batting side	*Pano* (from the Greek, 'up')
Bowler	*Bollerr*
Caught	*Apo Psila* (from the Greek, literally 'from on high')
Not out	*Ochi Sotto* (*ochi* = Greek 'no' *sotto* = Italian 'under')
Out	*Ow'dat* (applied both to the appeal and the umpire's response to it)
Stump	*Xylo* (Greek, 'wood')
Wide	Wide

*Play's the Thing, Darf Publishers, London 1988.

A peaceful study in green and grey of an olive grove. There are three and a half million olive trees on the island.

15 Olive Presses

Professor Augustus Sordinas, Ionian University

The visitor to Corfu walking amidst the vast olive groves or through the numerous villages of the island is liable to encounter large millstones or parts of gigantic wooden presses abandoned by the wayside. They are remnants of primitive mills and presses employed for centuries in the extraction of oil from the fruit of the olive tree. The buildings housing them are also mostly in ruins, though some are still standing.

The scientific study of the olive tree was pioneered by my late father, John B. Sordinas, who devoted his entire life to the study of the ecology and cultivation of this plant, and to the extermination of the many parasites and insects that are a constant threat to the olive crop. Later research added important insights to our knowledge of the olive tree and to the still unresolved problem of its domestication, and its diffusion throughout the Mediterranean and beyond.

The olive tree belongs to the *oleaceae* group which comprises thirty species, the most important of which are the *olea sativa* or *europea, typica,* or *communis,* and the "wild" variety, *olea oleaster* or *sylvestris.* We do not know exactly where early domestication of the olive tree occurred, but it may very well have been in the low hills of coastal southern Anatolia, including the Aegean region.

We have good evidence indicating that the production of olive oil beyond the mere subsistence level became important from the Greek Middle Bronze Age at least. Philologically speaking, Corfu could be associated with the island of Homeric Phaeacians, whose king presumably grew olive trees in his gardens. On the other hand, substantive evidence points to the fact that the effective production of marketable quantities of olive oil on the island became necessary only after the 16th century A.D.

Derelict olive oil press at Káto Pavliánas on the road to Paramona.

Interior of a ruined workshop of Káto Pavliána.
Twin presses of wood and iron and a wooden wind-lass in situ.
Photographed in 1975.

The exterior of the workshop standing in splendid isolation on the lonely road to Paramona.

A typical road-side olive-oil workshop at Kothoniki. It is part of the Sordina House and functioned during the 18th - mid-20th centuries.
Photographed in 1968.

This changed the economy of the island permanently and profoundly.

To understand the causes of this change - and the subsequent role of the olive oil workshops - we must turn to the history of the rise of Venice as the dominant power of the Adriatic sea and the islands and harbour of the eastern Mediterranean. Corfu is strategically situated in the centre of the Mediterranean and commands the Adriatic. This conferred upon the island all sorts of historical roles. Take, for instance, the role of Corfu as an outpost of the expansionist strategies of Venice since the 13th century (intensified with the Fourth Crusade) and, therefore, its indirect role in the rise of post-medieval commerce and city life. Precisely for this reason, the island was finally occupied by Venice for a period of four hundred years (1386-1797).

I have not yet determined what may have been the number of olive trees on the island prior to the coming of the Venetians. But production of oil must have been negligible - so negligible that in 1386 the Doge A. Venier did not even bother to include olive oil in his detailed list of taxable products.

Very soon the mercantilist Venetians determined that the soils and the climate favoured the cultivation and exploitation of the olive tree. They decided that Corfu should be forced to produce large quantities of oil for the enrichment of the *dominante*. To implement this policy Venice resorted to what amounts to an excellent example of "directed culture change". At first, in the late 14th century she started encouraging the planting of olive trees. But the results were negligible. Therefore, on September 28, 1565, an ordinance attempted to enforce the uprooting of vineyards and the planting of olive trees in their place. Yet the peasants - accustomed to what Pirenne has so aptly called an "economy of no markets" resisted the attempted change. Rejection was so intense that Venice resorted to the stimulant of fat premiums for each successful planting of 100 trees. Appetites were whetted. The economy of Corfu was quickly oriented toward an olive monoculture which ended up absorbing most of the labour and the commercial capital of the villages and the city until the end of the Second World War. Before the advent of tourism, 52.3% of the cultivable land was covered by olive trees. In 1960 there were 3,150,000 trees on the island.

Horse-drawn rotary mill with giant single millstone.

The economy of rural Corfu went through convulsions similar to those elsewhere symbolised by the cotton-gin, the sugar-mill, or the Brazilian mechanisms for coffee. Perhaps the only difference was that in Corfu these convulsions were painfully long-drawn. The merchants of Venice desired large amounts of olive oil but cared little about how it was produced. Few technological outlays were needed anyway because the olive is a fickle crop,

a slow and taxing procedure, needing mainly labour. And of this there was plenty. A large number of peasants switched their daily routine from horticulture or the many cares of the vineyard to the dull gathering of olives and the back-breaking production of oil.

The machines employed for the extraction of olive oil reflect, and in many ways describe, the activities involved, and tell us much about the various extraction techniques which slowly developed to meet the increasing production of olive oil. The location and distribution of these machines give further valuable information regarding the development of these techniques and of their relation to the settlement patterns. On the whole these aspects of the material culture of the island enable us to gain concrete insights into the behaviour of a very large segment of the population for the past three hundred to four hundred years.

We know a good deal about the production of olive oil in antiquity and about the most important methods employed for the extraction of the oil from the olives. The operation consisted of two distinct and separate processes, which in Corfu remained essentially unchanged until the end of the second world war.

The Mills

The first of these two processes consisted of the crushing or "pulping" of the fruit as a preliminary step to the extraction of the oil. This was done with various forms of gigantic horse-drawn rotary mills, the earliest of which, consisting of a single millstone, was replaced in the early nineteenth century by a more efficient type employing two or three smaller millstones.

It is strange but true, that these mills were, until the first half of the 20th century, more primitive than the *mola olearia* or the *trapetum* of classical antiquity. At present, some of them can still be seen in ruins, or abandoned amidst olive trees. But most are totally gone, often having been incorporated into the foundations of modern buildings.

The pulp that resulted from the crushing of the olives was placed in circular containers of local fibres - collected and plaited by the peasant women - to be subsequently pressed.

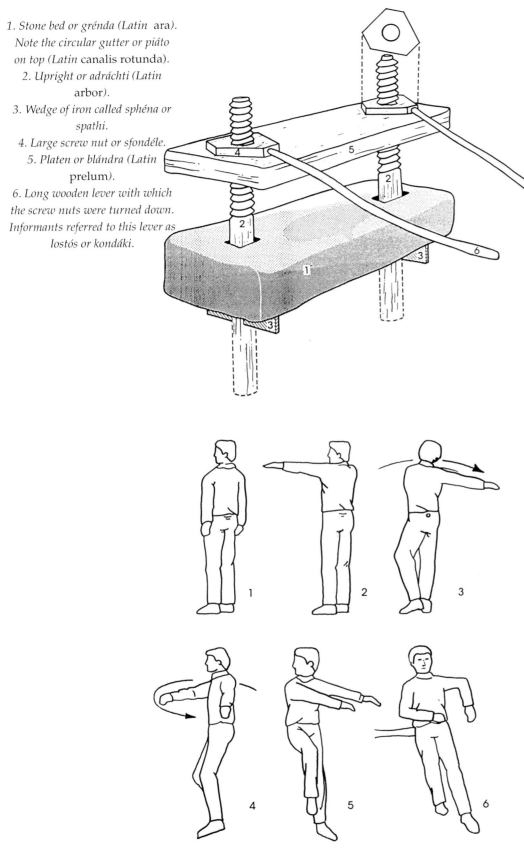

1. Stone bed or grénda (Latin ara).
Note the circular gutter or piáto
on top (Latin canalis rotunda).
2. Upright or adráchti (Latin
arbor).
3. Wedge of iron called sphéna or
spathi.
4. Large screw nut or sfondéle.
5. Platen or blándra (Latin
prelum).
6. Long wooden lever with which
the screw nuts were turned down.
Informants referred to this lever as
lostós or kondáki.

Opposite page.
Barrels brimming over with olives
gathered on the Sordinas estate.

The Presses

The second process consisted of the pressing of the pulp for the extraction of the oil. Various presses or parts of presses are known to us from Hellenistic and Roman writers, classical pottery representations and some classical and prehistoric sites. In spite of the impressive evidence, the reconstruction of these machines is not always complete or definitive.

The earliest archaeologically and ethnographically documented press in Corfu is a technological monster, still remembered by the very old as the "Åi" which is shown in the drawing opposite. It is an accurate reconstruction from pieces I found in various ruins during my 1968-70 research. Missing parts, as well as details about the operation of this machine, were obtained through oral reports. The operation of this monstrous machine was cumbersome, to say the least. It was normally operated by four men in teams of two working on the two levers which turned the two *sfondéle* nuts.

But all the males present in the workshop were invited to give a hand. "In the old days we slaved together", said my informants. Emphasis was on unison of motion. The men operating each lever worked in unison. The entire body of each operator acted harmoniously in a specific pattern of motions which we can follow in our drawing opposite. The men stood close to each other and a few feet away from the long lever of the "Åi" (No 1). Then in unison they extended the arms forward (No 2), gently twisted their bodies to the right, swinging the extended arms as far back to the right as possible, "to gain momentum", like ballerinas (No 3). Then, forcefully and abruptly swinging arms and body to the left (No 4), they lifted and extended the right foot forward (No 5) toward the lever - with the momentum gained - and yelling in unison "Åi" they "fell" together onto the wooden lever, striking it as strongly as possible with the right thigh (No 6). Under the impact the lever moved forward, the *sfondéle* nut tightened somewhat, and the awkward platen went down an inch or so, pressing the pulp underneath.

The act was repeated for hours. To give some protection to their hips and thighs, the labourers wrapped themselves with several sheepskins which were presumed to absorb the severe

shock caused by the full swing of the body against the cumbersome lever. It would be desirable to know what were the criteria of labour efficiency in those days. How forcefully should the labourer knock himself against the machine? Without unfortunately giving any details, a scientist in 1930 reports that hernias were customary, but were conveniently attributed by the workshop owners to over-consumption of olive oil. This masterful rationalisation is not devoid of humour and considerable ingenuity because, while it did nothing to discourage the strenuous effort, it warned against undue tampering with the precious oil supply.

In describing this idiotic operation, I cannot but wonder at the theoretical position of certain thinkers who deny the idea of progress. Once more we are reminded of Thomas Aquinas for his *Habet homo rationem et manum*. Undoubtedly, the latter is evidence in the ÅÍ press, but one wonders about the former. As might be expected, the ÅÍ press was very slow to operate. According to the majority of informants it required six to seven hours of continuous toil to press a load of pulp about 200 kgs, (which eventually produced 17-20 kgs of oil).

The early introduction of iron into the giant wooden olive presses.

In subsequent centuries, and clearly since the 17th century all sorts of presses were developed. The earliest ones (some in pairs) were entirely - and most admirably - made of wood. These were slowly replaced by iron presses. This did not happen overnight. At first, parts receiving the greatest stress were made of iron. Later, the entire press was made of cast iron.

To motivate these presses, wooden vertical windlasses were employed. They consisted of a pleasantly carved 2.5 metre tall cylindrical wooden drum about 25 cms. thick. A short horizontal handspike, inserted through a rectangular hole in the middle of the drum, enabled two men to turn a thick rope round the drum and motivate the press.

Stone vats were used for the preliminary storing of olive oil. It was transported to the city of Corfu in goatskin bags. Hence, the precious substance was transferred to large earthenware jars (not unlike the much earlier Minoan *pythoi*) to be shipped abroad - mostly to Venice.

The Olive Oil

Normally, with the arrival of dusk, the average peasant's toilsome day ended. Few lights were lit. Electricity did not exist, and burning paraffin was prohibitively expensive. The entire countryside was bathed in darkness except for a tiny olive oil lamp burning before the icons of the bedroom or an occasional shrine by the roadside.

Round 2 a.m., however, a couple of oil lamps were lit in the olive oil workshop and the embers of the hearth in a corner were kindled. The arduous day of the workshop had started - to continue uninterrupted until nightfall.

Olive oil - apart from its obviously nourishing qualities - was always held in great esteem. For centuries it was the only available fuel for primitive lamps. It produced a pleasing flame which has endured in the form of sacred lights in churches and synagogues.

The pharmacopia of olive oil is fascinating. Its curative powers have been legendary and have been praised for thousands of years.

In addition to all these, almost miraculous qualities, olive oil has been appreciated as a mild aphrodisiac. According to a well known Corfiot saying *fáe ládhi ki'ela vrádhi* which can be loosely translated "Eat some olive oil before our encounter tonight".

Be that as it may, make sure you sprinkle some of the gooey substance on your salad at lunch, that is before the evening's activities, during your sojourn on the somewhat problematical *"Venus of the Isles"*.

Shiny and colourful tools of the trade.

*Opposite page.
A gleaming basket of delicious black olives, the peasant's caviar.*

16 Traditions and Customs

Various Contributors

The traditions and customs of Corfu have a strong identifying link with ancient Greece. The line which joins the two leads back in an almost unbroken chain to early man and his fears when faced with the mighty strength of nature and the elements. Over the years human superstitions have undergone a subtle change, leading us to the customs of today handed down from generation to generation and owing more to magical, superstitious rites than to Christianity.

Let us begin with a few superstitions which originated in Corfu and some which also exist in other parts of Greece.

If wine is spilt at table, this brings good luck, although the opposite applies should you spill oil. One should never throw crumbs out of the window at night, as wealth will leave the house. You will receive money if your cup of Greek coffee has bubbles on its surface or if your left palm itches. Scissors or cupboards left open indicate that people are gossiping about you. If somebody sneezes during a conversation, it means that he is in agreement with what is being said. Never start a job on Saturday because, it is said, it may remain unfinished. Do not hand soap to a friend, as it means you will have a fight. If a house has two doors, a visitor should leave by the same door through which he entered.

A group of Corfiot lovelies line up in traditional costume.

Opposite page.
Study of a spinner of bygone days wearing traditional costume and jewellery.

CORFIOT CUSTOMS ON EASTER SATURDAY.

A custom which takes the unwary visitor by surprise takes place at 11 am, when in all the churches on Corfu the first Resurrection is announced with the words: *'Christos anesti'* (Christ is risen) to which the response is *'alithos anesti'* (truly He has risen). This is proclaimed amidst the loud pealing of church bells and the joyful sounds of the local brass bands as they parade through the main streets of Corfu town.

The oldest band plays a vigorous salute under the headquarters of the new band, and vice versa. Needless to say, each band competes with the other to see who can produce the most strident sounds. At this same moment, a shower of old crockery vessels are hurled down from top windows to crash noisily onto the street below. In bygone days cannons were fired from the old fortress, and until very recent times lambs were slain by having their throats cut in doorways, and the sign of the cross was smeared over the lintel with a bloody finger.

There are various explanations of the crockery breaking ritual. It is said to have originated as a punishment perpetrated on Jews passing below for having crucified Christ. However, this strongly contradicts the evangelical spirit of turning the other cheek. Another explanation has it that in ancient days crockery was always broken upon graves after burial rituals. Perhaps, in the same vein, the symbolism of Christ rising from the tomb should be also considered.

PROCESSIONS AND SAINT SPYRIDON.

In Corfu, great importance is given to the four annual processions in which the body of St. Spyridon, lying in its silver casket, plays the most important role.

The first of these processions is on Palm Sunday, and is in recognition of the miraculous deliverance of the island from an outbreak of the plague in 1629.

The second falls on Easter Saturday and commemmorates the relief of the island from famine in the mid-sixteenth century.

The third celebration takes place on August 11th, when the Saint was purported to have saved the Corfiots from a Turkish siege in 1716.

The final procession of the year falls on the first Sunday in November, as in 1673 St. Spyridon once again saved the islanders from a plague.

Numerous tales, both old and new, are told in town and village of the Saint's miraculous interventions - always in the nick of time - but these are far too numerous to list here.

HOW DO CYCLAMENS GROW?

Cyclamens, with their delicate aroma and pastel shades are called "Coppelules" or "Little girls" in Corfu. This name came into being through the following incident.

Centuries ago, a country priest had a beautiful young daughter who was as pure as she was lovely. One day the Venetian Governor of the island, well known for his dissolute life-style, caught sight of the priest and his child as they walked together in the town. Immediately the Governor decided that he must possess this girl. He forthwith sent his aide to find out who she was. Being pleased with what he heard, he followed this up by summoning the priest and his daughter to present themselves at his chambers. The poor priest, fearing that he had displeased the Governor somehow, made his way apprehensively to the meeting place. His fears were allayed, however, as the Governor welcomed them in a most hospitable manner and promptly invited them both to a lavish dinner where he saw to it that the priest drank most of the wine provided. When the innocent father eventually slumped over his glass asleep, the Governor took the young girl into what is now called the Old Fortress, ostensibly to show her around. As they walked, the heady combination of wine and desire overcame him and he embraced the girl who at once took fright and managed to escape his advances by running through the labyrinthian corridors of the fortress. As she ran, she could hear the heavy step of the Governor approaching. Soon, with his superior strength and knowledge of the building he caught up with her. In her desperate efforts to escape from him again, she slipped and fell from one of the sheer drops of the fortress walls. Her body was smashed on the stones below, killing her instantly. When she was eventually found, a soldier noticed a large pool of congealing blood on the ground under the corpse. Removing the girl's body, he covered the blood with earth and stones and placed two branches forming a rude cross on the spot.

Time passed, and one autumn the same soldier found himself again at the place where the unfortunate girl had lost her life. To his surprise he noticed an unknown flower growing exactly on the spot where he had placed the cross. Lifting the stone he discovered that where the girl's blood had once stained the earth a mass of beautiful flowers were growing. He immediately named them "Flowers of the Coppelula" and since that time Cyclamen in Corfu are known as "Little girls."

FOLK DANCES AND ENTERTAINMENT.

In Corfu the old dances used to bear the names of the areas where they originated. For example, 'The Kaiser's dance' or the 'Gastouriotikos' is derived from an Alsatian song whose rhythm coincided with that of a Corfiot dance from the Gastouri region. This is a lively dance, full of joyful leaps and good humour. It was first performed at Gastouri during the period before the first world war when the Kaiser lived at the Achilleion.

Opposite page.
A Corfiot beauty shows off her
colourful headdress and jewellery.

Orchestrated by the musicians of the Imperial guard, this is a circular dance with the participants facing in towards the centre and moving in an anti-clockwise direction. The female dancers hold each other by their little fingers, and the leader, a male dancer who invites the principal female dancer to perform with him is always a relative.

The leading woman dancer, in whose honour the dance is performed, holds in her free right hand a kerchief of bright colours, red being the predominant shade. The male dancer grabs one corner of the kerchief and signals the band to commence playing. As he dances he makes different movements with the kerchief, showing off his dancing capabilities in front of the other women. A second man stays in the background and dances mainly in front of the last female dancer. Occasionally he replaces the leading man, but only when he is given permission, and always providing that he is a person of trust.

When Kaiser Wilhelm occupied the Achilleion, he would often watch the dancers and said that this dance in particular presented an unusual and impressive picture which never failed to charm the onlooker. He was also quite convinced that this dance had originated in ancient times, and was a recreation of the ancient holy rites performed around the temples.

COSTUMES.

Amongst traditional costumes worn by women, the most spectacular is the one worn by peasants from the centre of the island. This is a most impressive costume, mainly because of its brilliant colours and decorative accessories.

A long sleeved shirt of fine linen with cuffs of heavy lace is teamed with a busk embroidered with gold birds, flowers and figures. The colours are light and dark shades of blue, red, mauve and maroon. A white linen petticoat peeps from below a skirt or '*fustani*' of pleated dark blue or black fabric which is worn with a silk apron, white or multi-coloured. White stockings draw particular attention to red velvet slippers heavily embroidered in gold, with large buckles. As a head-dress, a white kerchief is wound round the head and bound with a profusion of flowers and ribbons.

The corresponding man's costume consists of baggy trousers covering the knee, made of dark blue linen. A pleated white shirt is in handsome contrast to a double breasted blue waistcoat with two rows of silver buttons. An alternative waistcoat may sometimes be worn. This is in black with an intricate design carried out in gold thread. A short jacket, cropped at the waist and a red silk cummerbund with hanging fringes complete the man's attire. White stockings with buckled shoes are the traditional footwear.

CANTADES.

Cantades are melodious serenades arranged for many voices, and greatly influenced by Western culture. These songs have become a permanent and much loved part of Corfiot life, with their sweet tunes and romantic lyrics. In remote villages one comes across Cantades sung by local choirs who have had no formal training, but whose voices are nevertheless harmonious because of the Corfiots' naturally receptive musical ear.

SICOMAIDA.

Among the many unusual customs of Corfu, one must surely be the making of "Sicomaida." This sweetmeat is made from ripe figs gathered in August, cut up and dried in the sun then kneaded with fresh lees of wine. At a second kneading, aniseed is added with shredded almonds. The mixture is then shaped into flat round loaves and neatly wrapped in fig leaves and bound around with twine. It is then kept until Easter, when it is brought out as a dessert at fasting suppers during Lent and before major religious holidays after mass. Sicomaida is still sold today in Corfu. If you have the chance, sample a slice, the taste is unusual and quite delicious.

'VIVES'

The old custom of 'Vives' takes place in Northern Corfu. A close relation of the bridegroom gets up at the wedding feast and places a large glass on a tray. He fills the glass with wine and passes it round to every guest, asking each one to take a sip. The father-in-law of the groom raises the glass on high and wishes all future happiness to the newly weds. He then turns to the guests and greets them with the shout of 'Vives'. After drinking the toast down to the last drop, he replaces the glass on the tray, together with a sum of money for the musicians. During the entire celebration guests beat time rhythmically on plates with their spoons.

CARNIVAL.

An important and colourful part of local entertainment every spring was the Carnival.

Crude masks were worn, made from the rough skins of sheep or goats, with the hair still adhering to them. This was directly related to a custom left over from the ancient Dionysian rites, and was believed to ensure good crops and the delivery of healthy animals.

As time passed, the seven Ionian islands became influenced by European habits. Paper or fabric masks took the place of the old leather ones, and the custom of throwing confetti and streamers was added to the Carnival accessories, as were fancy costumes and the 'Domino', an all enveloping black cloak, often made of satin with a cowl-like hood which rendered the wearer completely unrecognisable.

In Corfu town, a popular Carnival practice was to satirise well-known personalities, such as, on one occasion, the members of the Municipal Council when they decided to pull down the Porto Reale, a decision which both the populace and the intelligentsia were against.

An early nineteenth century Corfiot peasant wearing a colourful red cap and sporting a paunch. Watercolour, Private collection.

Right and Opposite page. Elizabeth-Lulu Theotoky has devoted a significant part of her life to promoting the traditions of Corfu. As President of the Corfu Dance Theatre she aims to double the efforts being made to investigate and record for posterity details of local dress and dance in different areas of the island, and to make an effective contribution to the preservation of Corfiot culture.

These pictures show a group of Corfiot dancers in striking traditional costumes and girls captured in graceful motion by the camera of the well-known Italian photographer Gianalberto Cigollini.

During the Carnival period, some of the island's inhabitants danced far into the night garbed in fancy dress, while others chose to play in tavernas a peculiar and noisy gambling game known as the 'Mora'. Popular up until the time of the second world war, this left-over from the Venetian era was played by two pairs of men and the winner's proceeds were used to pay for the evening's liquid refreshments. A game of chance, the 'Mora', in which the two players try to guess the number of fingers which each has secretly displayed, is accompanied by much shouting as the bets were placed. If the game was played by Maltese workers brought to Corfu by the British to build the High Commissioner's palace, they would shout in loud sing-song voices.

Embers from the fire also found their place in Carnival ritual, especially for the game of 'Momolo' or 'Monkey Face'.

A small person, his face blackened with ashes, would hide inside an empty wine barrel left open at the top. Two friends thumped on the barrel, shouting: 'Come out, monkey' The little man would then poke his head out of the barrel, and making wild sounds and grimaces, frightened the watching women and children.

Many and varied are the tales told around a fire of a winter's evening, of half forgotten customs and traditions now only kept alive in the most remote villages.

As the visitor gets to know Corfu better, it is to be hoped that some of these old ways will become familiar to him, and life will become just that little bit richer.

Acknowledgements

Over the last two years, whilst I was putting together this book, a number of people have been very helpful. I am afraid that it would be rather difficult to mention them all. I will try, however, to include as many of those friends from London, Athens and Corfu as space here permits. My thanks and gratitude are extended to all of you who have made this publication possible.

I would like to start with Gerald Durrell, John Forte, C.C.W. Box-Grainger, Maria Hatzinasiou Makis Kalligeros, George Leotsakos, Spiros Lemis, Michael ("Gunns") de Navarro QC, Lord Orr-Ewing, Andrew Sinclair, Mary Stefanides and Admiral Themis Tsalas for their valuable help on a number of issues.

John Costopoulos, Chairman & M.D. of the Credit Bank A.E., John Karageorgis of Silver Carriers, Dionysis Livanos, Greek Minister of Tourism, Paul Psomiadis, Chairman of Aspis Pronia Insurance Company S.A. and the Management of the Cavalieri Hotel, Corfu for their generous and most valuable sponsorship.

Piero Curcumelli-Rodostamo, Bia Kritikou-Theotoki, Steven Manesi, Giorgio Marsan and Augustus Sordinas for allowing us to photograph their Estates, and Lady Holmes for letting us photograph her beautiful garden.

The Apergis Collection, Athens, the Archeological Museum, Corfu, the Averoff Collection, Metsovo, the Corfu Museum of Antivouniotissa, the Fine Art Society, London, the Gennadeion Collection, Athens, the Ghika Museum, Athens, the Illustrated London News Picture Library, the Photographic Studios of Kokali Bros, Corfu, the Kunsthistorisches Museum, Vienna, the Koutlides Collection, Athens, the Leventis Collection, Athens, Peter Nahum at the Leicester Galleries, London, the National Gallery, Athens, the National Galleries of Scotland, Pyms Gallery, London, the Reading Society of Corfu, the Hon. Sir Steven Runciman CH, Christopher Wood Galleries, London and all other private collectors for granting us their permission to include in this publication a number of watercolours, oil paintings, photographs and various documents from their collections.

Andrew Papadatos, the Librarian of the Reading Society of Corfu, for assisting us in gathering valuable facts and data from this important Library, Harper Collins Publishers Ltd for giving us permission to use extracts from Gerald Durrell's books Birds, Beasts and Relatives and Garden of the Gods and Rupert Hart-Davis for giving us permission to use extracts from Gerald Durrell's book My Family and Other Animals.

Loulou Theotoki, G. Chitiris and various other contributors for all the information obtained from their essays on subjects related to the Customs and Traditions of Corfu.

John Julius Norwich for reading the whole typescript and making many valuable amendments. While acknowledging this debt, the editor remains responsible for everything that appears in these pages.

Amanda Kalligeros, Anthy Koustoubardi and Sibila McGrath, my long suffering secretaries, for typing and re-typing hundreds of pages of illegible texts, Ken Reilly and his team at Precision Presentation for the design and production, and last but not least, my dear wife, for her invaluable help without which this book would not have been written.

Thank you all very much.